L.I.F.E. Guide for Men

Your guide to living free in sexual integrity

Dr. Mark Laaser

xulon PRESS

L.I.F.E. Guide for Men
by Dr. Mark Laaser

Printed in the United States of America

Library of Congress Control Number: 2002110004
ISBN 1-591602-53-X

Xulon Press
11350 Random Hills Road
Suite 800
Fairfax, VA 22030
(703) 279-6511
XulonPress.com

To order additional copies, call 1-866-909-BOOK (2665).

FOREWORD

Sexual dysfunction has become a common cancer within today's culture, and the church is certainly not exempt. The number of people struggling with sexual brokenness has sky-rocketed due to two main factors: the prevalence and availability of pornography and a sexually saturated media. Mark Laaser has commented that our entire society is being *sexually abused* by this onslaught. Unhealthy and un-scriptural sexual behaviors such as pornography, compulsive masturbation and adultery are just as prevalent within the Christian community as they are in the society at large. Among believers, there are men and women—including key leaders—who, because of painful experiences and sinful choices, compulsively use sex and unholy relationships as an escape to help them cope with life. Many of these same people desperately long to be free from their bondage and intensely desire to live in sexual integrity. They want to be Living in Freedom Everyday.

This "L.I.F.E. Guide for Men" is the first in a series of workbooks dedicated to helping God's people be free from the bondage of sexual addiction, and equipping them to walk in His unconditional love. Soon there will be L.I.F.E. Guides for women, for spouses, for couples, and for upper teen/student age young people of both sexes. L.I.F.E. Ministries is grateful to have Dr. Mark Laaser, an internationally known author and speaker in the area of sexual addiction for over 15 years as the author of this L.I.F.E. Guide for Men, and as the principal editor for the subsequent workbooks. Each of the L.I.F.E. Guides to follow will be written by known and respected experts in this area of ministry, with the close cooperation and participation of Dr. Laaser.

The L.I.F.E. Ministries support group program offers Christ-centered and relationally oriented groups that incorporate spiritual discipline, small group accountability and ongoing prayer and support to those struggling with sexual brokenness. L.I.F.E. Groups are support groups not therapy groups. While there is much within each of the L.I.F.E. Guides and the recommended recovery materials to help the struggler identify and deal with the wounds from the past, we also encourage individual therapy to address root issues and heal the woundedness that often leads to sexual addiction. The critical ongoing support comes from the networking together of lives in real relationships—open, transparent, and accountable connections with fellow strugglers. L.I.F.E. Groups value confidentiality, with an absolute commitment to a safe atmosphere for complete honesty; and complete acceptance, where members are embraced in an attitude of love and forgiveness by others sharing common struggles. All of this is "Guiding" the group members toward Christ-centered sexuality, under the conviction that our true sexual identity is found in the freedom and grace that only Jesus can offer.

REGISTRATION WITH L.I.F.E. MINISTRIES

We encourage all groups using this L.I.F.E. Guide workbook to become registered L.I.F.E. Groups. Registering your L.I.F.E. Group with L.I.F.E. Ministries International will entitle your group leadership to access additional information and discounted resources through newsletters and the L.I.F.E. Ministries website at www.freedomeveryday.org, and will open up additional communication links for information about conferences, workshops, leadership training and other benefits, often at substantial discounts. Your group leaders will have access to materials and information to help your L.I.F.E. Group grow and to expand your sexual addiction ministry within your church and your community. Your group will also be listed in our network of L.I.F.E. Groups, so those looking for help in your community can find it, and your group members will never be without needed support when away from home. Finally, by registering, your group will be furthering the work of L.I.F.E. Ministries International, and will help make this support group ministry available in additional churches and communities across the country and around the world.

To find out more, to start a L.I.F.E. Group, or to register your L.I.F.E. Group, checkout the website, www.freedomeveryday.org, call L.I.F.E. Ministries at **866-408-LIFE** (5433), or write for more information at the address below. Our mission is to encourage, empower and equip God's people to live everyday in sexual integrity. We would love to welcome you and start you on the journey toward Living in Freedom Everyday in His unconditional love.

L.I.F.E. Ministries International
P.O. Box 952317
Lake Mary, FL 32795

TABLE OF CONTENTS

ACKNOWLEDGEMENTS

From

Mark R. Laaser, Ph.D.

Writing a book or workbook for me is always a team effort. Such is the case with this L.I.F.E. guide for men. There are many people to thank who have significantly contributed to my thoughts, writing, and work on this project.

Ultimately, any work of this magnitude depends on the prayers of those faithful who support it. Most of all, I wish to thank Bob and Johna Hale for their tireless encouragement, "gentle" reminders, and unceasing prayers. They are true prayer warriors and it has been their vision all along that gave birth to this project and ministry.

Any author who spends hours at the computer screen must have the prayers, patience, and support of his family. My children learned long ago to "just let dad be," and to find other things to do.

Most of all, this book is dedicated to Deb. It has been her that taught me the true meaning of God's grace and sufficiency. Hers is truly the "face of grace, love, and forgiveness." It is more frequently her who practices what I preach, teach, and write. She has also been the source of strength to get through this. Finally, she contributed many of the ideas herein as she has gone to years of counseling, workshops, and support groups with me. More and more God is leading us into being ministry partners together and that is truly exciting.

A special word should go to Don Gleason who has really helped to shape the vision of our ministry and given both Deb and me a sense of where we are going in the next five years.

One special brother, Eli Machen, has shared in my ministry for over ten years. Some of the ideas in this workbook, like the whole concept of vision as it pertains to recovery, belong to him. I will always be grateful to Eli for his friendship, prayers, and support over the years.

Over the past years Deb and I have been partnered with Bethesda Workshop Ministry in Nashville, TN. I don't know of a more supportive local church than Woodmont Hills Church of Christ that sponsors that ministry. One of our colleagues there, Marnie Ferree is writing the workbook for female sex addicts. Her contributions to this series of work have been extremely helpful as is her leadership of that ministry. I also think of the counseling staff there, people like Angela Thompson, Ken Graham, and Richard

Blankenship. Sometimes just conversations with people like them has led to helpful ideas

There are many healing addicts who have contributed to this workbook by the insights they have shared as we all seek to find the discipline and answers to the challenge of being people of sexual health and integrity. For purposes of anonymity, they must remain anonymous. I think of Michael T. who really gave shape to the format of this workbook. I also think of the men of Faithful and True groups in places like Jacksonville, Fl., Rockford, Ill. and the Willow Creek group in Barrington, Ill. who have made many helpful suggestions. Thank you Jerry S., Walter H. and Mel A. Of course there are also the people of the original L.I.F.E. groups in Orlando whose prayers and suggestions are integral parts of the contents here. I must also mention all of our clients, workshop participants. There is rarely a day that goes by that I don't learn something from all of you.

Of course as not only an addict but as a co-dependent, I worry that I have left someone out or not recognized someone as deeply as I should. One of the greatest joys in my life is to share ministry. I hope that all who know me will accept how richly deep a part of my life you are.

Finally, if you are someone picking up this workbook for the first time, thank you for the courage it will take to get well. May God bless you.

Mark Laaser
September, 2002

ACKNOWLEDGEMENTS

From

L.I.F.E. Ministries International

Our deep gratitude goes to those who have also helped produce this work:

For the cover design, to Alberto Rivas for the original art work, and to Gail Halsey for the graphic design.

For their insightful and excellent editing and proof reading, to Jenna MacDonald and Bill Snell.

In addition, to the members of the L.I.F.E. Ministry leadership team, who have contributed not only hours of dedicated work, but the rich wisdom of their experience in support group ministry. Special thanks go to:

      Ellen D. for her inputs to layout and formatting;

      Rick J. for contributions to the sponsorship and accountability content;

      John E. for countless hours of overall supervision and his servant heart.

Of course, the greatest thanks go to Mark and Deb Laaser, not only for Mark's writing skill and dedication, but for their willingness to share the journey and all that they have learned from God about Living in Freedom Everyday.

L.I.F.E. Ministries International

September, 2002

L.I.F.E. Guide for Men

INTRODUCTION

Welcome to the journey toward Living in Freedom Everyday. I pray that this workbook will richly bless your life. Producing it has been a labor of love and is the result of the wisdom and generosity of many people. Not the least of these are the thousands of addicts and spouses that I have had the honor of working with over the last 15 years. But, mostly, it is the product of God's love and grace in many lives, including my own.

The foundations of this workbook, and the others in this workbook series, are the Seven Principles of Being Faithful and True. These were originally conceived when I worked with the American Family Association in 1997. The title, "Faithful and True," was taken from my first book and companion workbook.[i] It is the result of a conversation I had with Gary Smalley about what would be a more positive way of looking at the struggle involved in achieving or maintaining sexual fidelity. It recognizes that all Christian men and women seek to be sexually whole or pure.

Any of you familiar with the 12 Steps of Alcoholics Anonymous will recognize that the Principles follow the wisdom of those steps. It has always been my feeling that the 12 Steps contain much wisdom. Many Christians, however, have been reluctant to use them because they are not specific enough about our need to be in a totally dependent relationship with Christ. Therefore, we condensed the steps into seven principles and elaborated them in a language that is consistent with our faith.

This workbook will also introduce a new way of looking at what has for years been called "**recovery.**" This is the journey of freedom from old behaviors. We don't seek to recover old ways. But, we *do* seek to recover in that we *want* to get well. The freedom that we seek, however, is a matter of "**transformation.**" It is a journey that involves changing our lives. And, it is achieved through God's transforming power and love. Many of you familiar with the language of the recovery movement will notice that there are some ways that words change when we start thinking of the healing journey as transforming.

Over the years I have been immensely pleased when hearing about groups of men and women who have formed support groups for sexual addiction and have used my first workbook. Many of these groups call themselves "faithful and true." So why, then, do we need a new workbook? Our findings have been that because of the format of the original book, it was taking groups too long to get through the material. Many of the groups have taken up to a year to study through all of the lessons. Consequently, when a new member wanted to join the group, he often had to wait an extended period of time to get back to the beginning, and to the basic material that all people need to understand in the first days and weeks of the transforming journey.

These workbooks don't mean to necessarily replace that workbook. There is still a great deal of depth and power to the combination of material and Scriptural study. We have needed, however, a way to cycle through basic material in shorter periods of time. The design of this workbook and others in the series is that material can be studied in seven-week cycles corresponding to the Seven Principles. If you consider the outline, you will see that each principle has been divided into three main sections, or assignments. Each section goes increasingly deeper into the transforming journey of healing from sexual addiction. Intentionally, every person in a L.I.F.E. group can be working on the same principle in the same week. Some may be in the early days of their journey; others may have been working for weeks, or even months. The material is designed to meet individual need at varying times, while still focusing the group on one of the Seven Principles. Hopefully, working on this workbook will be like reading the Bible. Every time you do it, new thoughts and inspiration will come to you. If that is true, you will truly be able to use this material on an ongoing and indefinite basis.

This workbook really begins with my own story of sexual sin and addiction. It began when I was a boy and experienced sexual abuse, and it continued until I was 37 years old. Along the way, it included addictive masturbation, pornography, use of prostitution and sex with multiple women. The worst part of my story is that I abused the privilege of being a pastor and counselor by being sexual with women who had come to me for help. In a way, all of my writing is an attempt to make amends for the damage I did to my wife, family, and many others. Even though I had accepted Christ as my Savior early on as the son of a pastor, I never really surrendered my life to His liberating Lordship until I finally got sober. I had been beseeching God to change me, but I was really very spiritually immature and was trying to manipulate Him. I wanted what Alcoholics Anonymous calls, "a softer, gentler way." I spent a lot of my life being angry with God for not "fixing" me. I harbored deep longings inside my soul that I didn't know how to verbalize. I was lonely and angry – not only with God, but with many others around me. I had an active mind and was bored.

I sought counseling with many therapists and pastors. Since I was never fully honest with any of them, they couldn't help. Since they didn't, I had one more set of people to blame. My wife and I had what appeared, on the outside, to be a normal marriage. But really, we were strangers to each other, as there were many things about me that she didn't know. In essence, I led a "double life." I was a successful pastor, teacher and counselor on the outside, but I was a mess on the inside. Lust gripped me in ways that not even I accepted. And, I was in denial thinking that *I* could help myself if I wanted to. After all, who could I really talk to? To reveal my sins would bring consequences that I wasn't willing to face.

Finally, a group of angry people intervened on me. They had come to know about my sexual behaviors. They fired me from all of my jobs. They said that they loved me, but very few of them have ever talked to me since. There was one man in that group. He was a recovering alcoholic. The Holy Spirit, I think, came to him that day. I will never forget his words, "I think that your behaviors with sex are no different than mine with booze. If you trust me, I will find you some help." I was too tired to resist. I did what he told me to do. I went to a treatment center started by Dr. Patrick Carnes. Finally, I became honest with many people and started to heal. To this day, I am grateful for the pioneering work of Pat Carnes. Many of you will notice that some of what you will read in this book is based on his pioneering work. I am also grateful to a recovering alcoholic. In many ways my healing began with the pioneering work that Bill Wilson and Dr. Bob Smith started in 1935, a movement that became known as Alcoholics Anonymous (AA). Many of you will notice the obvious heritage of AA and its influence in some of these pages.

As I write this, I have 15 years of ongoing sobriety from sexual behaviors outside of my marriage. My wife and I have been married for thirty years. It is really only through her grace that I began to understand God's grace.   Along the way I may use elements of my story to illustrate various points. I do this not to tell you how wonderful I am that I have stopped all of those behaviors. It is only through the transforming power and love of God that I am alive. I use my own story in the hope that it might be an encouragement to you to know that *I am one of you*.   I don't write from some distant academic place. Like you, I'm also deeply longing for a more dependent relationship with Jesus Christ as I continue to seek Him in more dependent ways.

Most of all, I want you to know that complete healing *is* possible. When I "crashed and burned" and went to the treatment center, I thought that God was finished with me. Many people were angry with me. My story wound up on the front page of the local newspaper. My wife and I had no money. It was only then, in that brokenness, that we both really began to find the reality and healing presence of a loving, forgiving, restoring God. I had been too proud earlier. Now, in my total weakness, did I really come to understand that only *He* could do for me what I couldn't do for myself? Someone shared a scripture with me that became my theme verse during that early time. It is Philippians 1:6: "He who began a good work in you will be faithful to complete it until the day of Christ's coming."

Back then, in those early days, I never thought that I'd be writing any books. But, God has done some unbelievable things in my life. I hope that you find this workbook to be a place where your journey of healing and transformation begins. Please know that even as I write I am praying for you, and for you to know God in a more powerful way, as Christ completes the good work He began in your life.

How to Use This Workbook

Hopefully, you will be using this book because someone at a L.I.F.E. group recommended or gave it to you. You have made a decision to do something about your sexual addiction and have found a L.I.F.E. group. This means that you will have the strength of the fellowship of other men to help you get started. Lean on them and learn how to listen. Your own best thinking is what got you in this place. Quiet your mind.

Remind Satan that he has lost the battle with you, and that he should shut up too. You don't want to listen to him. You have made a firm commitment _not_ to listen to him again.

The first thing you will need to do is to obtain a journal of some sort. It could be as simple as a spiral bound notebook. It could be a fancy journal you can find at bookstores and office supply stores. It may even be a three-ring binder that you keep adding notebook sheets to. Whatever it is, your personal journal should be something that you feel completely comfortable writing in. We made a decision not to put a great deal of space in this workbook for you to write in. That is so you may refer back to its pages over and over again. You can copy some of it and give it to others. We want you to do most of the writing assignments in your journal instead of in this workbook, but we have provided some short-answer space here just for convenience. Each assignment will contain some amount of discussion about the principle being presented, and the thought processes necessary to complete the particular writing assignment(s) within that principle. We have clearly marked the actual assignment instructions within the larger discussion content to be sure you understand what you should record in your journal.

You should put your name on your journal. This now becomes _your_ **sacred** document. No one else should see it unless _you_ decide to show it to them. Do you remember how some of those old diaries had locks on them? Get that idea in your head. This is your journal. We want you to be completely honest in it. We don't want anyone else reading it uninvited.

We have seen, over the years, that others may want to look at your journal. Your wife may be one of them. Don't be hard on her for wanting to. She is petrified and hurt. She is wanting to know the truth. She is angry with you and may feel like she has the right to look at your journal. But hear me out: keeping the contents of the diary of your life is a healthy boundary you should not be afraid to set. The writing that you do in your journal is between you and God. Pray for the power of the Holy Spirit to help you.

You may at times want to show what you've written to your wife, to others, to your sponsor, group members, pastor, or therapist. It is acceptable if you feel it is for your benefit. Please know that it is your decision, OK?

Each of the Seven Principles is divided into three assignments. Every time a L.I.F.E. group meets it will focus on one of these principles. That principle will be the theme of that meeting. Every L.I.F.E. group, however, will have men in it at different stages in their healing journey. Some of the men may have years of sobriety. For others, it may be their first meeting. We intend for L.I.F.E. groups to always be open to new members who are coming for the first time. We can't predict God's timing as to when a person may finally decide to get help. Therefore, every time a L.I.F.E. group works on a principle, each man in the group should be working on one of the three assignments within that principle.

Each assignment is designed to take you deeper in the work of a principle. Assignment One will consistently be somewhat basic — it is the core and the foundation of that principle. Each Assignment Two will always ask you to work on the next core elements. Finally, Assignment Three will take you into deeper understandings of a principle. It is intended that you will work on the assignments in succession, but the idea is that you will work on all seven of the first assignments first, then all seven of the second assignments, and finally all seven of the third assignments. That means that after completing Principle One, Assignment One, you will move on to Principle Two, Assignment One. When you have completed Principle Seven, Assignment One you will then go back to Principle One, Assignment Two, and so forth.

You might want to put a chart in your journal that looks something like the one below. You can use it to check off how you're doing.

THE SEVEN PRINCIPLES

PRINCIPLE	ONE	TWO	THREE	FOUR	FIVE	SIX	SEVEN
ASSINGMENT ONE	WEEK 1	WEEK 2	WEEK 3	WEEK 4	WEEK 5	WEEK 6	WEEK 7
ASSIGNMENT TWO	WEEK 8	WEEK 9	WEEK 10	WEEK 11	WEEK 12	WEEK 13	WEEK 14
ASSIGNMENT THREE	WEEK 15	WEEK 16	WEEK 17	WEEK 18	WEEK 19	WEEK 20	WEEK 21

Remember that you will be working **across** this chart. Principle One, Assignment One is the first work you will do. Principle Seven, Assignment One is the seventh work you will do. Principle One, Assignment Two is the eighth work. Principle One, Assignment Three is the fifteenth. Finally, Principle Seven, Assignment Three is the twenty-first work you will do.

There are a total, therefore, of twenty-one assignments. This does not mean that you will just need twenty-one weeks to do all of the work. It may take you several weeks to do one of the assignments. The important thing to remember is that you can work at a pace that is comfortable for you. Your sponsor or your group will help you to know how you're doing. Remember that at each meeting you will be working on an assignment related to the principle being discussed that night. This could technically mean that you could work several different times on the same assignment, but that those times could be seven weeks apart.

Let's assume for example that you are working on Principle One, Assignment One. You start on this the first time your L.I.F.E. group is addressing that principle. The next week you will move to Principle Two, Assignment One. You may not be completely finished with Principle One, Assignment One. You can come back to it. You just keep going. By this understanding it could possibly take you a year to work through the entire workbook for the first time. Others of you, being impatient, may want to march right through and get all the work of an assignment done in one week. It will therefore take you twenty-one weeks to get through the entire workbook for the first time.

Everyone is different. This workbook is a living, breathing document. You may work through it a number of times in the course of your healing journey. As you will notice, there are other suggested readings along the way. You can always add to your work on this workbook with the help of other books and workbooks. I certainly don't claim that this workbook is "exhaustive." It is the most complete workbook that I am aware of, but it is only one book. More and more, we are seeing ministries publish similar materials. Never consider that you have to be "loyal" only to this workbook. A workbook is a tool. It is for your benefit. If there are other materials that help you with your healing journey, that's great; use them to support your journey to freedom and healing.

The main thing to remember is that your L.I.F.E. group will concentrate on the Seven Principles of staying sober. I have seen that rigorous and thorough work is the best way to start healing. Finally, you may start filling more than one journal or notebook, and that's OK. Journaling is one of the best emotional and spiritual tools there is, and working in this workbook may just be the start of this great spiritual discipline. You may already know that many great writers journal regularly. As you read and study Scripture for the rest of your life, writing your thoughts and feelings may become like a friend, one that helps you grow continually.

Please don't hesitate to call someone at L.I.F.E. Ministries International if you find yourself not understanding what to do at any time. Your local group should give you a list of phone numbers. You can always ask another "journeyman" who has been doing this for some time to help you. As you progress, you will become more comfortable with the idea of asking for help.

Most of all, I pray that the God of all peace and understanding will keep your heart and mind focused on Christ Jesus throughout this journey.

Meeting Guide

In this chapter we will present guidelines for holding a meeting. First of all, we recognize that since this whole series of workbooks is being sponsored by L.I.F.E. Ministries, most of the support groups which use this material will call their groups "L.I.F.E. Groups." We also recognize that there may be other groups that use this material. There has been a network of "Faithful and True" groups across the country. Some of those groups may choose to identify themselves by that name, but I encourage you to become a L.I.F.E. group in order to help support this work across the country and around the world. There may also be groups around the country that call themselves by a variety of names. It is not as important what you call yourselves as much as it is how you conduct your meeting. We expect that all groups calling themselves "L.I.F.E." or "Faithful and True" will follow our meeting guidelines and leadership principles.

Others can use this material. Some Christian therapists could use the material in these workbooks if they want to conduct a therapy group. In such cases, the meeting guide will not be necessary, as therapists will competently know how to conduct a group. We do not encourage individuals to use this material. As you will see, it is intended for fellowship and not isolation. That does not mean, of course, that you won't do most of the work within the workbook alone. It should only be done, however, in accountability with others in some way. For the remainder of this chapter, we will refer to groups as "L.I.F.E. Groups."

Every L.I.F.E. Group should follow a standard format. Our experience has been that meetings that don't use a standard format can often become a free-for-all. They are vulnerable to the moods and distractions of the moments. They may also be vulnerable to the more dominant personalities in the group. We know that all groups will need strong leadership and that a few individuals in every group will provide that. It is not fair to them, however, if only one or two always have to lead the group. There are times when those who seek to dominate the groups are the least healthy in the group. If the safety guidelines listed below are followed, this should not become a problem. We suggest, therefore, the following outline. Each group or leader may want to modify the outline to best suit the group's unique needs, but I ask that you modify with care, as once your format is established, your group will need to stick to it consistently.

Meeting Format

1. The group leader starts by saying, "My name is _____, and I am healing from sexual addiction. This is the (State the time of the meeting, e.g. the Monday night) L.I.F.E. Group, and I welcome each and every man. I commend you on your commitment to remaining sexually faithful before God."

2. Opening prayer. The leader prays or the group, saying a group prayer of their choosing. Many groups might choose the serenity prayer or the Lord's Prayer.

3. Group Introductions. Go around the circle with everyone introducing himself as the leader did, "my name is _____, and I am healing from sexual addiction."

4. New Members. New members are welcomed. The leader says, "We're glad you've come. On your first night you are not expected to talk, but we will be honored if you do. There may be opportunities for you to provide input either in this larger group session or after we break up into smaller groups. But most importantly, for you as a newcomer, this is a time to listen and start feeling safe. We believe that we all need a sponsor to help us work this program, so if you would like a temporary sponsor for the next week(s), see me after the meeting. Also, if you have any questions about our group and how it functions, please also see me after the meeting."

5. Someone will read the Mission Statement, or a part of the Mission Statement, the Seven Principles, and/or the Seven "Cs" (all printed below).

6. Someone will read the Safety Guidelines (printed below).

7. Offering. The leader says, "All L.I.F.E. groups are self-supporting. We pay for our own materials, rent (if applicable) and other expenses, and we contribute to the L.I.F.E. Ministries International. We suggest $5 weekly as a contribution to your own healing, and to help ensure that others have access to the help that you have found. Like an offering at a church, you are not required to give; and you are certainly free to give more." An offering plate (or envelope) is passed around the group.

8. Business. The leader leads the group in any discussion of old and new business. Old business can include matters such as meeting times and places and ordering of materials. New business can include matters such as special but related events outside of the group or any announcement of matters pertaining to the group's well being. Note that all decisions are made through the consensus of group members. All decisions must be consistent with the policies of L.I.F.E. Ministries. When in doubt, check with the national office.

9. Someone will have been asked to either make a presentation or lead a discussion on the principle being discussed that night. This should be limited to no more than 20 minutes.

10. Celebration of Sobriety. All members are encouraged to report-in about their success and talk about how long they have been sober. Recognition of significant periods of time should be noted such as one week, one month, three months, six months, and one or more years. The group may provide some kind of memento, such as medallions or certificates, as recognition of these achievements.

11. Small groups. Depending on the size of the group, everyone counts off in such a way as small groups are created, each consisting of four or five men, including the small group leader. The small groups meet for about one hour, 20 minutes, and each should be led by someone with appropriate experience and sobriety. The time is divided equally among the members, using the outline below. This is a time of accountability, confession and building relationships.

12. Closing. The whole group reconvenes. The leader thanks everyone for coming and reminds everyone of the next meeting and of any other L.I.F.E. meetings that are locally available that coming week. He may also say, "If there is any unfinished individual business, make an appointment with your sponsor or accountability group for a meeting this week". Someone will then read The Hope (printed below) and the group will say a prayer together. Each group will choose a closing prayer. The leader should then invite interested men to remain for prayer among themselves, while being sure that the formal meeting adjourns on schedule.

The timeline for a standard meeting of a little over two hours might look like this:

Welcome, opening prayer, and introductions	5 minutes
New Members, Mission Statement, Safety Guidelines	10 minutes
Offering and business discussion	10 minutes
Principle presentation and discussion	20 minutes
Celebration of Sobriety	5 minutes

Small Group
> *Feelings check in*
> *Bottom lines*
> *Top lines*
> *Getting current*
> *Story time (time for part of a member's story or testimony – 10 minutes)*
> *Prayer requests*
> *Prayer*
> *(Small group time equals no more than 10 minutes per person)*

Total Small Group Time	60 minutes
Reconvene and closing	5 minutes

The Mission

Ours is a fellowship of Christian men who have a sincere desire to abstain from sinful sexual behavior. Many of us have been trapped in the vicious cycle of sexual addiction. Ours has been a life of sexual fantasy, ritual, sexual sin and despair. We have felt out of control. We know the words of Paul in Romans 7:18-19, "I know that nothing good lives in me, that is, in my sinful nature. For I have the desire to do what is good, but I cannot carry it out.   For what I do is not the good I want to do; no, the evil I do not want to do -- this I keep on doing." Our sin has grown worse over time. We have been addicted to the high of our lust. We have not been able to stop despite the consequences that have come to us.

Ours is a history of broken promises, violated vows, families broken apart, jobs lost, physical pain, financial chaos, spiritual bankruptcy and even death. All along what we truly sought was love and nurturing. We have been angry because we felt unloved and that our needs weren't being met. We have even been angry with God because He didn't take away our lust. We have been bored with ourselves, with life, and with each other. We substituted sex for love, thinking that the high of sexual pleasure would erase the true needs of communion with God and relationship with Christ as well as with others.

Many of us have promised, "This is the last time I will act out," but it was not. Don't be discouraged. You are not alone. Those of us who have chosen to become honest about our pasts and our emotions are experiencing healing with the help of the Holy Spirit. Many of us have tried to recover through our own thinking. We have even tried to manipulate God's healing through constant prayer, Bible studies, and church attendance. We found that God will help us heal only if we are truly willing to submit to His will by keeping ourselves humble and accountable.

Following are the principles we follow as a path for healing the wounds of our sexual sin.

Seven Principles of being Faithful and True

1. *We admit that we have absolutely no control of our lives. Sexual sin has become unmanageable.*

2. *We embrace a belief in God, accept the grace offered through Christ, and surrender our lives and our wills on a daily basis.*

3. *We make a list of our sins and weaknesses and confess those to a person of spiritual authority.*

4. *We seek accountability and to build our character as children of God.*

5. *We explore the damage we have done, accept responsibility, and make amends for our wrongs.*

6. *In fellowship with others we develop honest, intimate relationships, where we celebrate our progress and continue to address our weaknesses.*

7. *As we live in sexual integrity, we carry the message of Christ's healing to others who still struggle, and we pursue a vision of God's purpose for our lives.*

For some of us it has been easier to remember these principles in the form of the following seven Cs:

   1. Conceit is gone.
   2. Control is surrendered.
   3. Confession is made.
   4. Character is changing.
   5. Contrition is offered.
   6. Consistency is established.
   7. Communicating "the hope" is essential.

These principles are a guide on the journey of recovery and not the magical cure. If you are willing to give up your old way of thinking and the years of behaviors you have used to medicate painful feelings, then you too can become and remain sexually whole.

Because we come from different Christian backgrounds and traditions, we do not endorse any particular church or denomination. We have no opinions concerning race, economic background, politics, philosophy, or differences between persons as long as they claim Jesus as their personal Savior. What we share is a common desire to be totally honest about ourselves, about what we have done, about who we are and how we feel, and to remain sexually whole. We define sexual wholeness as the ability to be sexual solely through the expression of emotional and spiritual intimacy in heterosexual marriage. If you sincerely and humbly share this desire, we welcome you in this fellowship.

Safety Guidelines

It is absolutely essential for every L.I.F.E. group to be safe. Safety produces the environment in which people will feel most compelled to be honest. Read the following guidelines at each meeting. All group members will be responsible to help see that they are observed. If they are violated, confront each other in love. If a group member cannot observe them consistently or after being confronted, please ask that group member to leave the meeting. The well being of the entire group is always more important that any one person in it.

1. It is safe to be honest. We expect all members to tell the truth.
2. It is safe to have feelings. All feelings are acceptable to God and to us.
3. We will allow group conversation. We are allowed to give each other feedback as long as it only reflects our strength, hope and life experience. We should begin our feedback with "I," and not with "you." We do not seek to give advice.
4. There will be no preaching. Messages of spiritual strength and hope can be shared, Scripture can be quoted and theological statements can be made. We should avoid statements that use words like "should, always, never, God says, God's will for your life is, or God will be angry if..." L.I.F.E. Ministries does not endorse any particular religious denomination or group. We all seek to follow Christ in our own way.
5. There will be no shaming of yourself or others. We will not put ourselves or others down.
6. We do not seek to blame anyone for our sinful behavior. We take total responsibility for our actions.
7. Group confidentiality will be observed. We will never reveal the identity of other group members or any other personal information outside the group — even to our spouses. **There is only one exception to this rule**. If any member of the group discloses feelings or actions that reflect that he is a possible danger to himself or to others, including children, we will take all necessary action outside of the group to report that danger, and to ensure the safety of the individual and any others around him. Even more specifically, any disclosure of past or present unreported child abuse must be reported. **We need to be very clear on this point**.

The Hope

If we are truly humble and broken,

If we have truly surrendered our lives to Christ,
If we have confessed the exact nature of our sins,
If we continue to grow in our relationship with the Lord,
If we seek to become men of integrity,
If we continually seek to correct the sins of our past,
If we remain constantly in accountability with God and with others,
And...
If we search for ways to spread this message of hope,
Then we have many things to look forward to:

We will know that God loves us for who we are and that He has sent his son to die for
us.
We will be able to accept God's grace and forgive ourselves.
We will accept that others love us regardless of who we are and
what we have done.
We will stop equating sex with love and nurturing.
Our lust will diminish.
Fear of others finding out about us will stop.
Fear regarding money will cease.
Anxiety regarding the future will begin to fade.
We will learn how to make healthy choices.
We will become more in touch with all of our feelings.
We will heal from the wounds of our past lives.
We will be able to be more intimate with spouses and friends.
We will be better parents.
We will come to know and praise the Lord in ever increasingly meaningful ways.

Is this an unbelievable hope? We think not. Our lives are testimonies that God is
working in us, sometimes quickly and sometimes slowly, always toward His greater
glory.

Please join us in the closing prayer.

Definitions

Communication is essential to intimate fellowship. Fellowship is vital to living in freedom everyday. Group discussions, feedback and presentations are the life-blood of support and encouragement. We must learn to understand and listen to each other. Each L.I.F.E. Group will need to speak the same language. There should be as little confusion as possible in regard to terminology used. I suggest, therefore, that each group member study the following definitions. Discussion can focus on them. The definitions are based on my understanding, having traveled around the country and talked to hundreds of people in the process of healing. Every group, however, may have local or personal understandings that are important. The main point is that the group be willing to discuss meanings so that everyone can be clear about them.

90 Days

This comes from the AA slogan, "90 days, 90 meetings," and refers to the first three months of healing. It can be necessary for a person go to one meeting every day for the first 90 days in order to remain sober. This can be true for sex addicts as well. Ninety days has also been applied to the period of time a sex addict may choose to pursue sexual abstinence with self and others, including the spouse. You will find more information about the concept of ninety days of abstinence in Assignment One of the Accountability Chapter, Principle Four.

Abstinence

This is the state of being non-sexual with self or others. Abstinence should not be confused with being "celibate," which is the state of not being married.

Accountability Partner

This is any person who agrees to be in your network of people holding you accountable. A common mistake is made thinking that you can have one accountability partner. I have never known a person to recover when they have only one. One of your accountability partners can be your *sponsor* as defined below, but your spouse should not be one of them. The word "partner" may describe that there is more mutuality in this relationship than a sponsor would be.

Acting Out/Acting In

Acting out refers to sinful or dysfunctional sexual behaviors. It could also refer to any sinful or dysfunctional behavior. "Acting in" refers to rigid control of sexual behaviors in an unhealthy way. It may mean that sex (or some other behavior) is being avoided but emotional and spiritual growth has not been achieved. "Acting out" and "acting in" are really opposite ends of the same continuum. They can both be attempts to control painful memories or emotions. "Acting in" can be synonymous with sexual anorexia.

Addiction

Historically, the word "addiction" has been controversial in the Christian community. Some fear that using it takes away personal responsibility for any sinful behavior. Some have felt that those who call themselves addicts often use the word addiction to blame it for their own personal decisions. All truly humble and repentant addicts that I have known, however, always accept personal responsibility for their actions.

The medical and psychological community has several universal criteria for determining if a substance or a behavior is an addiction:

1. **Use of the substance or behavior has become "unmanageable."** This means that the addict has intended to stop, over and over again, but can't. There will be a history of failed attempts. Some would say that there must be a two-year history, at least, of an unmanageable pattern present for a person to be labeled an addict. The word "powerless" has also been used to describe this pattern. Sometimes addicts refer to themselves as "out of control." One way to consider this, also, is that an addict creates destructive consequences for himself by sinful behavior, but even this has not been enough to get him to stop.

2. **The addiction gets worse over time.** This means that more and more of the substance or behavior will be needed over time to achieve the same effect. An alcoholic knows, for example, that over time more and more alcohol will be needed to get "high" or drunk. Sex addicts know that more and more sexual activity will be needed to achieve the same "high" of the acting out experience. This can take two forms. The most basic is that more and more of the same kind of behavior will be needed. I have known, for example, people who start masturbating once a month and progress to once a day or more in the course of their addiction. For some addicts progression will mean that they will need new kinds of acting out experiences to achieve the high. We must be careful to remember that many addicts will not progress to illegal, highly dangerous, or sexually offending kinds of behavior. Some do, but the majority do not. Sexual addicts may be able to stop their behaviors for periods of time, but until they find healing, will always return to them. Over time, a pattern of repeated failure will be present.

3. **Medical science is beginning to discover that there are reasons in the brain for the factor of progression. It is called "tolerance."** The chemistry of the brain can adjust to whatever an addict puts into it. Over time the brain will demand more to achieve the same effect. For alcoholics, the brain adjusts to alcohol and more will be

needed. Thinking about sex and engaging in it requires that the brain produce the brain chemistry to achieve sexual response. New research experiments are finding that the sexual chemistry of the brain can also become tolerant. This would mean that more and more thought or activity will be necessary to have the same brain chemistry effects — the feelings of arousal, excitement and pleasure. In many ways, sex addicts are drug addicts, the drug being produced is in their own brain.

4. **Because of the brain chemistry involved, addicts use the thoughts and behaviors that produce it to either raise or lower their mood.** We say then that addicts "medicate" their feelings. If an addict is depressed, lonely or bored, he can think of exciting sexual encounters, either remembered or imagined. The arousal part of the sexual response produces chemicals that raise mood. If an addict is stressed, anxious or fearful, he will tend to think of the relationship or romance quality of the encounter. These chemicals create a feeling of well-being and contentment and can, therefore, lower the mood. Most addicts are capable of both kinds of thoughts and can, therefore, both raise and lower their moods depending on their feelings at the moment.

5. **Finally, addicts act out despite negative consequences.** They have either already experienced them or they fear them in the future. Addicts don't pay attention to negative consequences and are in what is commonly called "denial." This can also be called "minimization," or "rationalization." When addiction progresses it usually leads to different kinds of consequences. Until a decision is made to surrender control of the fears that prevent addicts from getting help, they will continue to act out. Addicts may also continue to act out because it is usually a slower form of suicide. They know they are destroying their lives but their depression prevents them from caring.

Bottom Line

A "bottom line" is a boundary. It can refer to the distinction between which behaviors are tolerable and which ones are not. An addict may have a bottom line as to what sexual behaviors are outside of his/her sobriety definition. A spouse may have one about which sexual behaviors would cause him or her to leave if they happened again. Bottom lines can also be referred to as a "line in the sand." There are several Twelve Step fellowships that refer to bottom lines as "inner circle" behaviors. The inner circle is the place where all behaviors that are not allowed are included. So, if an addict says that his bottom line says that no masturbation is allowed, he might also say that masturbation is in his inner circle.

Boundaries

Most simply put, boundaries are guidelines for safety. Boundaries define what behaviors should and shouldn't occur in relationship and in families. They **pro**scribe what behaviors should not be allowed. When these boundaries are violated, we say that it is "invasion." They **pre**scribe what behaviors should happen. When these boundaries are violated, we say that "abandonment" happens. We often say that some people have nonexistent or "loose" boundaries. They will always allow themselves to be harmed in some way. We also often say that some people have too high or "rigid" boundaries. They won't allow themselves to be loved or nurtured. There are many people who don't know how to establish their own boundaries. They might be co-dependent. There are many people who don't know how to observe another's boundaries. They might be perpetrators of harm or abuse. Stating your boundaries should be a way of asking for safety. This can be different from making "demands." A demand is a request for more immediate action. That may have more to do with fear and anger than it does with a request for safety.

Co-Dependency/Co-Addiction

These two terms are often used synonymously but there can be subtle distinctions. Co-dependency was first used in the Alcoholics Anonymous (AA) community to refer to anyone who was in relationship with an alcoholic. The assumption was that these individuals tolerated drinking because they remained in the relationship. This assumption led to them being considered dependent on the alcoholic. And, since the alcoholic is dependent on alcohol, they are co-dependent on alcohol. It is felt that this tolerance of an alcoholic and his/her drinking behavior is based on the fear of being alone. It is, therefore, more important for the co-dependent to maintain the relationship than it is to confront drinking and the problems it creates. In the development of understanding about many other addictions, including sex, all those who seek to understand how they tolerate problematic behavior have adopted the term co-dependent.

From this basic definition, many have written about co-dependency and said that co-dependents abandon their own needs and attend to the needs of the addict. They are more interested in maintaining the approval and presence of the addict than they are in speaking the truth. This can cause them to seemingly ignore their own needs and wants and sacrifice themselves. This is a sacrifice out of their fears and not out of their strengths.

Co-dependents often "enable" the addict, making excuses for him or her and generally looking the other way. They also perform many of the tasks that an addict should be responsible for. This has led many to term co-dependents "doers." Accordingly, all that co-dependents "do" may save addicts from consequences, which often earns them the title of "rescuers." Finally, since co-dependents seem selfless, some have called them (and they may see themselves as) "martyrs." Essentially, co-dependency is a fear- and anxiety-based disorder in which the individual has an addiction to approval.

Co-addicts are people who are in a ***primary*** relationship (such as marriage) with an addict. They may or may not suffer from the symptoms of co-dependency. Some co-addicts may not be consciously aware of their partner's addiction. They may seem strong and self-assured, but some feel that this, too, can be a disguise for insecurity.

Please be aware that like any label, we use this only for the purpose of identification of the problems that need to be healed. We should always seek to use them in love and not in judgment. Some primary partners (spouses) really reject labels such as these. They find them too humiliating. They might say, "It's his problem, not mine." The main question to ask after expression of feelings like these is "What has kept you in the relationship?"

Compartmentalizing

In James 4:8, the brother of Christ says that we can be "double-minded." This means that various parts of our brain can be at war with each other. This is certainly true of addiction. Paul, in Romans 7, says that we don't always do what we want and that we often do what we don't want to do. This can be due to the fact that we "compartmentalize." We segregate parts of ourselves off and are not "unified." This can refer to "dissociating." This means trying not to focus, concentrate, or think about something that is painful. We, thus, compartmentalize it and then deny that it even exists in reality.

Cross Talk

This simply means talking back and forth at meetings — the process of feedback. Some groups have struggled with this concept because certain members of a group can talk too long, give too much advice, be too angry or judgmental, or simply be rude. People are encouraged at meetings to be good listeners and to not be amateur counselors. Members should always seek to be loving in their feedback. We feel that cross talk is essential to meetings as it provides support. See the safety guidelines in Chapter One.

Cruising

This term can refer to any ritual behavior (see Principle One, Assignment Two) designed to find a partner to sexually act out with. As such, it can refer to a variety of behaviors a person does to find and attract a partner. Dress, or appearance, facial expressions, what car you drive, and where you "hang out" can be included in cruising. In same sex cruising it often means your "looks," or your "glances," or even your tone of voice.

Cycle

A cycle is when one thought or behavior leads to others that eventually lead back to the original thought or emotion. The sexual addiction cycle is explained in Principle One, Lesson Two.

Denial

Simply put, denial is avoiding or "denying" reality. It is usually fear of consequences that causes one to avoid the truth. The consequences that are feared could be the reactions of others or the reality of emotions. Denial involves both direct lies and the avoidance of the truth.

Entitlement

All addicts need to "excuse" their behaviors. They search for reasons why it is "OK" to act out. One of the main excuses is called "entitlement." This means that the addicts "deserve" to act out. Some addicts keep a balance sheet in their head and feel that when they have done enough good behaviors, they can do some bad behaviors. In other words, they are entitled. Some addicts feel so unfairly treated in life (martyrs) that it would be only fair to get something for themselves. Anger and narcissism are usually behind the feeling of entitlement.

Family of Origin

Your family of origin generally refers to your immediate biological family. This would mean your parents and brothers and sisters. It can also mean any people who have lived with you under the same roof. This can mean stepparents, uncles, aunts, grandparents and cousins, but it can also mean others who lived with you, even if they were not biologically related to you.

Fantasy

Fantasy is thinking about anything in an imaginary way. Sexual fantasy is imagined sex and can be about past experiences or about "hoped for" experiences in the future. Jesus said that even though it may just be sexual fantasy, it is still adultery (Matt. 5:28).

Intimacy Disorder

This is based on the core beliefs "I am a bad and worthless person," and "No one will like me as I am." These are foundational to sex addicts and co-addicts. Those who suffer believe that if they tell the truth or express their real emotions, the other person will not like them or may even end up hating them and leaving. This often means that the people whom they are most afraid of losing, like their spouse, will be the people to whom they are less likely to tell the truth. Intimacy Disorder is a fear- and anxiety-based disorder. The fear is that someone will leave them and the anxiety is that they will be all alone.

Medicating/Pharmacological Management

Medicating refers to using a substance or behavior to alter a person's mood. Some substances and behaviors can elevate mood, as in the case of loneliness, depression or boredom, and some can depress mood, as in the case of stress, anxiety or fear. Medicating has been called "pharmacological management" in that the person manipulates his own mood, becoming like a pharmacist of his own brain.

Minimizing

Similar to denial, and really a form of it, minimizing literally means to attempt to make smaller what is really true. It is most often used when a person tries to minimize the effect destructive behaviors have on himself and others.

Narcissism

This is a clinical term that is more commonly used to refer to self-centered behavior. The figure of Narcissus was a Greek figure that loved looking at his own reflection. "Narcissists" often congratulate themselves on their own accomplishments or give themselves a wide variety of compliments. They seem to be thinking only about themselves and not about others. Their own agenda is the most important. They can seem very grandiose and self-confident or self-assured, but they really are not. They are very concerned about others' approval. Usually, they have been "narcissistically wounded," that is they have experienced a variety of different traumas in their lives. These traumas have damaged their sense of belonging and of being worthy. Narcissists really lack self-confidence and are trying to give it back to themselves.

Neuro-chemical

All activities of the brain are facilitated by the interaction of chemicals in the brain. What is sometimes called the electrical activity of the brain is based on chemistry, or "neuro-chemistry." Scientists have identified hundreds of chemicals involved in the process of one brain cell "communicating" with the other. Some people are born with genetic predispositions to having problems with the proper balance of these chemicals. Addictive and dysfunctional behavior can also alter the normal state of brain chemistry. Psychiatry is the medical science that seeks to understand the right balance and which can prescribe medications to correct such a disorder.

Objectification

This literally means b view someone who is fully human as an object that is not. Sexually, objectification means to view someone as only a physical body and not as a person with a mind and soul. It is, therefore, easier to lust after someone as just a body to be desired.

Rationalization

This is an excuse or justification. Rationalizations are used when one is trying to explain why he should do or have done something.

Relapse

This is a series of slips that reflect that emotional, spiritual and sexual boundaries have been crossed. Sobriety is being violated in an ongoing way.

Rubber-Necking

This simply means turning your head to take in a sexual stimulus, mainly another person, for a longer period of time.

Sexual Anorexia

Like anorexia about food, sexual anorexics avoid sex. Another clinical term can be "inhibited sexual desire," or "disorder of sexual desire." Painful memories (conscious or unconscious) shut sexual desire or availability down. Anorexia is often about anger and/or anxiety. Sexual addicts can be sexual with others and anorexic with their spouses. In these cases it can be guilt, shame, anxiety or a variety of other factors that shut them down.

Shame

One of the core beliefs of sexual addiction is, "I am a bad and worthless person." This is shame. Shame is not inherently bad. There can be "healthy shame." This is felt when a person knows that he needs God. "Unhealthy shame" occurs when a person's life experiences, like trauma, lead him to believe that he doesn't deserve God's love.

Sobriety

Most simply in terms of Christian morality, a state of sobriety exists when a person is not being sexual with self or others that he is not married to. Any sex outside of marriage is a violation of sobriety. So also is any sexual behavior used to medicate negative emotions, whether within a marriage or not. As Jesus said in Matthew 5, this can include thought life or fantasy.

Slip

This is a one-time violation of sobriety in any form. I like to think of it as an acronym meaning a **S**hort **L**apse **I**n **P**rogress. It remains a slip only if the person learns from it, repents and grows in understanding as a result.

Sponsor

A sponsor is the person who is your main accountability partner. The qualities of a sponsor are described in Principle Four, Assignment One. While you will need many people in your accountability group or network, there will be one person who more or less takes charge and helps you direct the show. This person will help you plan your healing journey, meeting attendance, phone calls, counseling and spiritual direction. He will not do all of these things, but will help you monitor how you are doing in the program. You will need to "submit" to your sponsor's authority and will need to determine what consequences will be appropriate if you fail to honor your commitments to healing.

Trauma Bonding

This is one of the trauma reactions that is described in Principle One, Assignment Three. It is commonly used to refer to dysfunctional attachments and unhealthy relationships. It means that two people are attracted to each other because of conscious and unconscious characteristics that remind each other of earlier people in their lives that wounded them. The hope is that by attaching to this kind of person, a new chance will be had to heal the old wounds. This is basically the hope that if you keep repeating old behaviors you will eventually get it right. It can also mean that you hope this time to be more in control, reversing the roles, and now you have the chance to be the one with the power.

Trigger

There are two basic kinds of triggers in our program. Any sexual stimulus that is seen, heard, felt, smelled, tasted, remembered or fantasized about that creates sexual desire or action (even if only in the brain) is a **sexual trigger**. It is generally assumed that the word trigger refers to the stimulation of inappropriate sexual desire or action. Any stimulus (in the variety of ways just described) that creates emotional and spiritual feelings of anxiety, fear, loneliness, boredom, depression or anger is a **general trigger**. Often, general triggers are also referred to as "emotional triggers." General triggers become sexual triggers when sex is used to medicate the feeling that general triggers create.

There are many triggers that we consciously know about. Looking at pornography can trigger sexual desire. An attractive person can do the same thing. Some memories of past sexual experiences (sometimes referred to as euphoric recall) can trigger sexual thoughts. Music, such as a particular song, can accomplish this. There are other triggers that may be more unconscious. They can be based on life experiences that we don't always consciously remember. Certain words or actions, certain expressions or tones of voice, certain times of the year or events, certain music and certain sexual behavior can all trigger emotions or reactions. One key is to discern if at any time your emotional reaction seems out of proportion to the event taking place. When that happens, your unconscious memory may be taking you to old places that you don't always realize. Have you ever had someone say to you, "You're overreacting?"

A Final Word On Words

Words are words. I have seen definitions and understandings change over the years. It is never a good idea to argue about definitions. Words are tools to help us communicate. Definitions are not something to live or die for. Come to a group consensus on them and move forward.

In addition to the few that I have defined, your group may encounter new ones or many others that I have not included. Please contact us with ones that you might like to know about, have a good definition for, or simply think should be included in future editions of this workbook.

Principle One

We admit that we have absolutely no control of our lives. Sexual sin has become unmanageable.

Confronting Reality: I'm Shackled in My Own Prison

Congratulations! Despite long years of deceit, lies, self-denial, minimizing, fears, shame and manipulation, you have come to a meeting. You have been wanting to, thinking that you perhaps should, wondering if it was the right thing. You have resisted, found excuses not to, wondered who would find out, and worried about the consequences of getting honest. You have thought that no one would really understand. You have either thought that you have done the worst things possible and that no one else has ever done them, or that your stuff is not so bad and that you really don't need to come. Hear these words:

Welcome.

You're in the right place.

We're glad you're here.

Imagine what it must have been like for the Prodigal Son. He just wanted to be home. He didn't think that he deserved to be in the same status as before because his sins were so great. He just wanted to be like one of his father's hired servants. Maybe you're like that, you are simply glad to be alive and able to get to a meeting. You'd just like to be here and be quiet and belong. The Prodigal Son's father, however, rushed out to meet him and prepared a great feast. That is what it is like with God. We want to be "imitators of God, just like little children." You've just arrived on the bus or entered the lunchroom or ventured onto the playground. We rush over to greet you. We've been where you've been. We're glad you've come. There won't be a great feast but we can go to coffee later.

Your first assignment is to just get honest. We know that the greatest enemy of sexual fidelity is silence. We want you to tell us how bad it got and what it was like to feel powerless over your life. You are now going to confront those demons in your mind that are telling you, "No! I can't talk about that. Someone will go running and screaming out of the room if I reveal all of that." There is nothing, certainly no sexual sin that separates you from the love of God. Chances are that others in your group have done some of the same things. The assignment that you are about to undertake will take great courage. It will be a risk, but, it is worth it.

Assignment One - Admitting Our True Condition

Unhealthy sexual behaviors have been variously divided into categories and groups of categories. In his first book, Dr. Patrick Carnes grouped such behaviors as shown in the chart below. As you look at these, note the behaviors that you have struggled with and to what degree, even if you were only involved with a particular behavior once. Try to remember how many times you have done each of these. You may have to estimate. No one remembers, for example, how many times they have masturbated. State how often this most recently took place (once a day or more, once a week, and so on). If you need further explanation of the categories, try reading Dr. Carnes' book, Out of the Shadows. My book, Faithful and True, also divides sexual behaviors in this way and defines each one.

Basic or Building Block Behaviors	Began	How Often
Fantasy	____	____
Masturbation	____	____
Pornography	____	____
(magazines, videos, Internet, TV, books, movies, music)		
Prostitution	____	____
(on the street, over the phone, in massage parlors, escort services, on the Internet)		
Affairs	____	____
(long-term and emotional involvement, short-term and non-emotional, one night stands, sexual or non-sexual)		
Anonymous Sex	____	____
(the name of the sexual partner is not known)		

Paraphillic or Level Two Behaviors	Began	How Often
Voyeurism	____	____
(undressing someone with your eyes can be included)		
Exhibitionism	____	____
(wearing provocative clothing counts)		
Indecent Liberties or Frateurism	____	____
(hugging someone and getting sexually excited is included, as well as any form of touch performed for a sexual feeling. This is true even if the other person isn't aware of it)		
Phone Sex/Cyber Sex	____	____
Bestiality	____	____
Sado-Masochistic (S&M) or Pain Exchange	____	____

Offending Behavior	Began	How Often
Incest	____	____
Molestation	____	____
Rape	____	____
Authority Rape	____	____
(using the power of role, status, age, or authority to gain sexual access)		

Every addict has made various promises and attempts to stop. List some of the times you have made such attempts and the actions you have done to stop your sexual behaviors. Make sure to list the most recent ones.

What is your earliest memory of being sexual? How old were you? Was there anyone else involved?

Plot a timeline of your life; perhaps as a vertical line down the left margin of a page, with your age marked to the left at different intervals from your earliest years at the top to the present at the bottom. In the space to the right, note the times when the frequency of certain sexual behaviors increased and when new forms of sexual acting out occurred.

What consequences have you experienced?

Think of various categories such as those below, and note when they occurred by entering the answers to these and other questions at the appropriate point on your timeline:

Financial	*How much money have you spent? How much money has this cost you?*
Physical	*Have you contracted any STDs or AIDS? Have you been sick in any way that is the result of the stress of your addiction? Do you experience any sexual dysfunctions (impotence, premature ejaculation, lack of desire)?*
Social	*Have you been divorced or lost a relationship? Is anyone really angry with you that won't talk to you? Have you had to move from a certain place? How are various members of your family with your history?*
Legal	*Have you ever been arrested, spent time in jail, or been sued?*
Vocational	*Have you lost a job or lost time at work? Are you underemployed or not able to work in the career of your choice?*

Addicts act out when they are tired, lonely, angry, anxious, sad, afraid or bored. Often these emotions work in combinations. Can you recognize times when you acted out when you felt these ways? If so, describe a time when this was true.

Some of you may turn to other resources to work through this material. Assignment One parallels the work of the *Faithful & True* workbook, Unit 7: lessons 1-3, and Unit 8: lesson 1. You may also find similar work in the other workbook listed in the resource section. Finally, some of you may be familiar with 12-step materials like the SA "White Book." For this assignment you would include any work that you have done surrounding step one.

Now, writing all of this information in your journal is one thing — it is a step toward being honest. But it is not the final step. Ask yourself, how long you have kept this information to yourself. What lies have you told to cover up this story? It is a story, isn't it? It is a part of who you are. It doesn't define you, but it does belong to you. For years you have been thinking, "If people knew this part of my story, they would hate me and leave me. They wouldn't want to be around me." Your feelings of fear have been your oppressor. They have kept you hostage. Your silence has been the result. Silence has been your companion. Lies have guarded your silence. Loneliness has become all too familiar. You have had two lives, the one that others know, and the one that only you know. The public one may have many friends, but the silent one has none. Your silent self pervades and overwhelms all else in the darkness of your loneliness. It is time for your two selves to unite.

The only way to do that is to break the silence. That is what your group is for. They are the brothers who will stand with you. They won't go running and screaming out of the room. They have done many of the same things you have. They will understand. Confront your fears. Be of good courage. Share the story. Your group will give you a chance to do so in the group setting. You may not tell all of it the first time, but eventually you must. You may want to practice with one or two members of the group first. You will find a tremendous sense of relief in doing so.

Congratulations! You are beginning the journey of transformation, of living in freedom everyday.

Assignment Two - Understanding Our Cycle

In this assignment you will continue to look at your history, that silent self that has kept you in bondage. The purpose of this assignment is to continue to bring into the light that which has been in darkness. It is also to show you some things that you will need to work on in a very specific and practical way.

Dr. Carnes first described that addiction follows an addiction cycle in his book, Out of the Shadows. *I have also defined it in my books. You may want to check these out for more thorough explanations and features. Briefly outlined, it looks like this:*

Fantasy is defined as all of those thoughts that you have about sex. It has also been referred to as "preoccupation." You have been preoccupied with sexual thoughts and fantasies. The next lesson will help you to understand more about your fantasies and what they mean.

Sexual thoughts lead to **rituals**. We seek to get ready to act out sexually. Any thought or behavior that you use to get to acting out is part of your ritual. The following questions will help you define what that is. AA (Alcoholics Anonymous) calls the following kinds of thoughts "stinking thinking."

What have you told yourself about why it is OK to act out? As a Christian you have had to justify why it is possible to disobey the commandments. For example, we might think that if we do enough good things for God, it allows us to do a few bad things. It's like we have a balance in our heads — a formula — and we say to ourselves, "God won't mind if I do these sexual things because I did so many other good things for Him." I used to think that because I was a minister and did many acts of Christian service, God wouldn't mind the "other stuff."

> *Have you ever thought these things? Write in your journal about any justifications you've had.*

Sometimes we justify our sexual sins, thinking that we deserve it. We call this "entitlement." Down deep we're angry about not getting our needs met. Many of us have said to ourselves, "Nobody loves me and no one will take care of me, I have to do it for myself." The most obvious justification involves thinking about your spouse, "She doesn't understand me or take care of my needs. If she were just more sexual or available, I wouldn't need to do these things." Maybe some of us hold on to the belief that being in a marriage will end all of our sexual lust. We have read I Cor. 7 in which Paul says that we should get married so that we don't burn with sexual lust. This belief tells us that it is our partner's fault or that we've married the wrong person. We then feel justified in the sexual sins we commit. It is anger on our part to do so.

> *Write down in your journal if these kinds of thoughts have ever been true for you.*

Entitlement also tells us that we do so much, we are so stressed, and we deserve to get some needs met. No one else seems to be doing it, no one else understands. Life is a problem. We might even think that it is only fair to do these sexual things. Have these kind of thoughts ever been something that you've said to yourself?

Remember that acting out is usually an expression of our anger. We are lonely, yes, but it takes anger to get most of us past our moral and Christian beliefs.

> *Make a list of those people in your life that you know right now you're angry with. Next to each of those names, write down what you're so angry about.*

Take as much time as you need to and just ask God to help you. Remember that you may also be angry with God. King David was. Many of the Psalms were written out of his anger with God. Study I Kings. *Who else was David angry with?*

Name	Reason(s)

Once we have justified our sexual sin somewhere in our mind, the next step is to prepare for acting out. One of the great challenges of healing and building a new life is to intervene on these "preparations." Following are a set of questions to help you identify those.

First of all, select the sexually sinful behavior that you have done the most. Write it down in your journal. Now remember the last time you performed that behavior. If you can, and you may need a friend in your group to help you talk through this, back up in time to the point you first start thinking about doing it. From that thought, what did you do next? If, for example, you have looked at Internet pornography, start by thinking of the last time you did that. Retrace your steps to the moment you first started thinking about going online. Did you need to wait for private time? Have you arranged for a private account? Do you do it late at night? Do you have a secret code or screen name? Do you have a separate credit card to pay for this or a post office box to receive bills? The possible list of how you might have set this up is endless. Some of the qualities of it might be totally unique to you.

Write this down in your journal.

Repeat this process for any sexual behavior that you have engaged in. Start with the most common ones first and then progress to the ones that you may even have done only one time. Having an affair might be an example of that. Some affair rituals take weeks or months to develop. They move from the first time you saw your affair partner, through initial conversations, to various acts of connecting before sex even happened. It has been said that those who have long-term affairs cross many emotional and moral boundaries before they ever cross sexual ones.

Write this all down in your journal.

Have you ever "traded" one sexual behavior for another? Many of us have thought that if all we did was to masturbate or look at pornography it was a real "moral" victory because it stopped us from doing something more serious. Some of us said, "I'm not going to have an affair, I'll just masturbate." Some have also said, "I won't have an affair, I'll look at pornography or go see a prostitute. Paying for sex is not as serious as having an affair." These kinds of thoughts also qualify as ways you have justified sexual sin. We all tend to "rate" the severity of sin. We might tell ourselves that we are not as bad as some other guy who does "worse" things.

Think and pray about how you were feeling going into your ritual. Were you lonely, stressed, frightened, angry or anxious?

> *For every different kind of sexual behavior, write down, to the best of your ability, how you were feeling when you started your ritual.*

This may take some hard thought and conversation with your brothers. Have you ever found that the excitement of just being in the ritual is enough to "medicate" the feeling? You may find that different kinds of sexual behaviors have different feelings going into them. For example, you may find that feeling stressed or anxious may lead you to look at pornography and masturbate while anger may lead you into more serious forms of sin.

It is one thing to say to yourself that you want to stop a particular sin. It is more complicated to say that you want to stop your ritual behavior. **One key principle to remember is that once your ritual has started you will act out eventually.** It is therefore imperative that you create a plan to stop the ritual behavior. It is time to conceptualize what those prohibitions will be. Go back to the ritual that you described in question one or two. What behaviors will you have to stop to avoid being in the ritual? For example, a man who rents X-rated videos will have to avoid the bookstores which sell them, possibly the neighborhoods in which they exist, alone time in the car that might take you to those neighborhoods, and the money in his wallet to pay for them. This sounds harsh and very restrictive, but in the early days of establishing sobriety, it is probably necessary. In another example, a man who has affairs will have to avoid one to one conversations with any women he is not married to. This sounds unfriendly, but probably necessary in the early days. These prohibitions can be amended as strength is achieved. I talk to other women, but I would never go out to lunch with them by myself (this being a part of my old ritual). For now, make a list of behaviors and tell it to your group.

Ritual Behaviors:

_____   _____
_____   _____
_____   _____
_____   _____
_____   _____
_____   _____

As I said, rituals lead to acting out. You have already worked on acting out behaviors in Assignment One. The last stage in the cycle is the stage of despair or depression. Dr. Patrick Carnes discovered years ago that almost 75% of all male sex addicts have contemplated suicide. Guilt and shame are part of this desperate feeling.

> *In this next part of Assignment Two I want you to simply write or journal about the most depressing time of your life that you can remember. What was that like? What do you remember? Have you ever thought about suicide?*

You may find that you want to be evaluated for clinical depression. That means that you will need to see a medical doctor like a psychiatrist, or a counselor to assess your level of despair. Go back and read the story of David for how he reacted to his own sexual sins. He was a desperate and depressed man.

As you see in the cycle diagram, sex addicts seek to relieve their sense of despair by altering the feelings involved with it. They will return to the high of sexual fantasy and the cycle repeats. It is also important for some of us to recognize that some also turn to other behaviors that "medicate" the mood. Roughly half of all sex addicts are alcoholics or chemically dependent. Many are smokers, hooked on caffeine or other "normal" drugs. Some turn to behaviors like work, sports, TV watching or spending. We now know that many sex addicts have multiple addictions. It is common for many alcoholics, for example, to discover after they have months or years of recovery that they are sex addicts. In the journey of your healing, you may need to deal with other substances or behaviors that you use to alter your moods.

One of the ways I have looked at it was to remember how my family taught me how to avoid my feelings. We liked to watch TV, eat, smoke, play or watch sports, shop, work and go to church. My dad had scriptural answers for everything, and that isn't a bad thing, but it did serve to help us at times to avoid what we were really feeling. It will take you some weeks of sobriety from sexual addiction to recognize some of these other behaviors.

> *For now, make a list of other addictions or problems that you think you have.*

Now take a grace break. Remember that we are all sinners and stuck in the cycle of our own sinful thinking and behavior. Even Paul admitted that he didn't do the good things he wanted to do and did do the things that he didn't want to. He said, "Oh what a wretched man am I!" Why do you think that God sent his Son to earth, because we were perfect? God simply asks you to lean on Him more and more each day, one day at a time, and begin to understand how much He loves you. Remember again the story of the Prodigal Son and focus on how the father rushes out to meet his son. God is watching for you to come home and He is preparing for a feast.

Assignment Three - Identifying our Roots and Desires

As you have worked through the principles you should now have a pretty good grasp on how truly powerless you have been over your sexual addiction. **You should have at least three months of sobriety before you take on this next assignment.** As you begin, you may have already noticed that many feelings have come up for you that you have historically sought to medicate.

Stop for a moment, this may seem like a problem to you. Perhaps you have been one of those Christians who has believed that once you start making the right decisions, like getting sober, everything will just automatically get better. You may have thought that you wouldn't experience negative consequences, that your spouse would just start trusting you, that you wouldn't lose your job, or face financial chaos. Most of all, you have thought that you would be "happy."

The period of time between the third and the ninth month is a really dangerous time for a variety of reasons. The first is that you might be experiencing the violation of expectations that were just described. This might lead to anger on your part. You might say to yourself, "What's the use of being in a healing journey if this is all I get?" You could be angry about all of the restrictions in your life now. There seem to be so many things that have been taken away. You may have feelings that you are not normal, you are now an "addict" and you feel strange. You may also be getting tired of all the hard work.

Relax. You are normal. Remember that even though you call yourself an addict now, the word addict doesn't define who you are. You are a precious child of God. You are fearfully and wonderfully made. You really are a person who has suffered with an addiction, but you are much more than that.

In the first part of this assignment make a list of the good qualities about yourself. If you can't think of any, ask some of your group members to help you.

Now that you have reminded yourself of good things about yourself, you can move on. Don't forget that you need to work your program just as hard now as you did in the first few weeks. It is time to go deeper into your thoughts and feelings. It is time to get to some of the root causes of your loneliness and anger.

Please start by doing some reading in other places about family of origin. There are a wide variety of places to do so. Check out the resources listed on the L.I.F.E. Ministries website at *www.freedomeveryday.org*. If your group wants to be on the same page, read through chapters 6 and 7 of my first book, *Faithful and True*. These chapters will give you an idea of how families work and some of the mistakes they can make.

Since I originally wrote that book, I have come to some more complete understandings of how we should think about our family of origin. We used to make the distinction between coming from an unhealthy or dysfunctional family and a healthy or functional family. That put many of us in a rather difficult position. Many of us had a hard time with this. We thought that we came from a rather nice family. We may have been rather protective of them and really not wanted to get into all these memories of problems. This is a rather natural resistance. We have been taught as Christians to love and honor our families. We do in fact love them and probably need them.

I've decided that our thinking in these matters gets too black and white. Do we really need our families to be either "good" or "bad?" I believe that all families are families that do many good and loving things and that all families make mistakes. I know that I've made many mistakes as a father. Does that make me a dysfunctional dad? I hope that it makes me a father who loves his kids and tries his best. I believe that is true of those parents in life who make horrendous mistakes. Some of them are immature and selfish even to the point of really terrible things happening, but as you will see as we outline the healing journey, we shouldn't get stuck in trying to decide how good or bad they are. That is ultimately up to God to decide.

In my experience, some of us have felt what I have come to call "family of origin shame." This can take two different paths. One of them is to think that we come from the worst possible family. Our story is really bad, our parents really terrible, and wounds really damaging. We might even be tempted to think that it is no wonder we committed so many sexual sins — our history is just a nightmare. We can also get competitive in thinking that our story is the "worst." The other path is to feel shame because we really can't think of that many bad things that our family did. Now we're in trouble. How could we have committed terrible sexual sins, when there doesn't seem to be any root cause? Those of you who feel this way start worrying that the problem is really you and that thought is really shameful. We might even start thinking about "inventing" some stories about our family so that we can "fit in."

Even the therapeutic community is concerned about this last possibility. There is a debate that goes on about something called "False Memory Syndrome." The belief by some is that therapists can help a person create memories that didn't really happen. For example, if a therapist has ever said to you, "80% of all sex addicts are sexual abuse survivors, you must be one too," you might need to be careful.

Over the years I have found that the best approach is always the way of prayer. As you begin this assignment, take a moment every time you work on it and ask God to help you remember the events of the past that you need healing from. Tell God that you are willing to heal them and that you are not just looking for excuses. Tell God that you have a lot of pain, loneliness, and anger and you are wondering where it comes from and then ask Him to show you. Always be in counseling or in groups that remind you to engage in this kind of prayer. Therapists, pastors and groups can only guide and encourage you in this prayerful journey; they can't suggest to you what really happened.

My first workbook, *Faithful and True*, contains writing exercises and explanations in units 9 and 10 to help you work through understanding your family. Remember that any work that you do is for the purpose of understanding. Some of you may work through this kind of material with a therapist or pastor who counsels.

Let me summarize some of the issues that you should be aware of:

- The rules that existed in your families. Think of examples of how your family taught you to express your feelings, to talk, to accept responsibility. Or did your family not talk, not feel, blame, minimize or deny responsibility?

- Did your family observe healthy boundaries? Did you feel safe? Did you feel loved, protected, nurtured and affirmed?

- Were there addictions present in your family? Some of these might have been substances, and others might have been behaviors.

- If you felt that you were emotionally, physically, sexually or spiritually abused in an invasive way, give examples of how that happened.

- Do you feel that you got what you needed? Were you affirmed, heard, praised, kept safe, touched, desired and did you have meaning modeled to you? If you feel that you were deprived of these things, have you perhaps dealt all your life with being lonely? It is hard to give examples of times when you didn't get something because something didn't happen. Can you describe times when you did feel lonely, left out, different, strange or weird? Can you remember times when you felt frightened? Can you describe times of feeling that no one cared or wanted you? Can you remember times of feeling that there was no meaning in your family?

Writing Assignment: I am asking you to delve into feelings that you might be resistant to remembering or having. Create, if you can, an image in your mind. Do you remember the story of the little children being allowed to come to Jesus after the disciples had tried to keep them away? Imagine that you are one of those children. You really want to sit on Jesus' lap. There is something keeping you from doing so. Then let yourself hear Jesus say, "Come to me." When you climb up on his lap, imagine that He comforts you, tells you that He loves you, and then that He asks you, "What are you feeling? What is it like to be you?" Remember, you are a child. Be honest with Jesus. What was it really like? He can hear you and understand. He already knows what it was like for you. He wants you to say it.

Write in your journal what this conversation with Jesus was like.

The principle of why we do this hard work is simple. Painful memories have a way of surfacing in our minds and creating feelings. Have you ever had someone, like your spouse, say to you, "You're overreacting," or "Why did something so trivial create such a large reaction in you?" Sometimes, these reactions come in other forms. You may think that someone is angry with you and they believe they're not. Do you ever find yourself suddenly getting sad at some song, movie, TV show, or event that no one else around seems to be getting sad about? Likewise, do you ever find yourself getting angry at something and it just doesn't make sense? Of course, there is the big one, has your spouse ever said "no" to your sexual advances and it created huge reactions of anger, resentment or pain in you? These are all possibilities of older feelings affecting your current reaction. We say that any stimulus that brings up feelings that are much older to the event is a "trigger."

Recently, for example, I was at the funeral of a woman who was the mother of one of my best friends. When they closed the casket I felt intense feelings of sadness and started to cry. Now, I hardly knew this woman. What it reminded me of is the death of my own mother. She died four years ago. My sadness was for her. Over the years there are many things that I notice that trigger me into my sadness or anger about my mother. For example:

> When one of her favorite hymns is played
>
> When I see a woman who acts or looks like her
>
> Crossword puzzles (one of her favorite things to do)
>
> The month of February (the month in which she died) and anything about the month like the events of the month, the temperature outside, snow, etc.
>
> My wife saying no to sex
>
> Anything any woman says that suggests rejection to me

This is a partial list but it does give you examples of how broad and how trivial these triggers can be. Do you get the idea? If I'm in a conversation with my wife, for example, about many different subjects and my old feelings are brought out, they can affect my reaction to my wife. They really belong, however, to my mother.

Here is an important principle of being faithful and true:

> **Heal your oldest feelings first, later feelings will follow, and your healing journey will be more successful.**

Current issues that you are having may be the latest evolution or manifestation of wounds that you have known since childhood. We have a way of repeating old issues, hoping for healing, and being frustrated when they never seem to go away. This could be true in your relationships. If you argue with a spouse, friend or anyone about superficial issues, you will probably stay stuck in repetitive fights, angers and resentments. Those relationships that are able to go deeper are generally the ones that are able to heal.

Writing Assignment: We all have a variety of ways that we cope with feelings. Some of us may avoid them at all costs. We may use addictive activity to medicate those feelings. In his book, *The Betrayal Bond*, Pat Carnes talked about eight reactions to our wounds that are possible. You may want to read that book as a group to get a more detailed description of these. Ralph Earle and I also listed these in our book, *The Pornography Trap* (pps. 86-88). For now, let me list them briefly.

1. Blocking	*This would refer to any behavior or substance that you use to change how you're feeling. You've already thought about sexual behaviors and to some extent, other substances and behaviors. Don't forget those socially acceptable substances like caffeine in addition to ones like nicotine and alcohol. This time make sure that you also include what would be considered as "positive" behaviors (like work). Sleeping a lot is another example you may not have thought of. The effect of blocking is that you're "numbing" yourself. I often refer to this as "going to the land of numb."*
2. Splitting	*The clinical community refers to this as "dissociating." When you split, you "leave." You may be lost in thoughts, daydreaming, or even having fantasies. (does that sound familiar?) Rape victims are known to leave their bodies and emotionally go someplace far away. It is like that for some trauma survivors, their minds go far away.*
3. Abstinence	*This means that you avoid any stimulus that would remind you of the trauma. Some sexual trauma survivors, for example, might avoid sex altogether. This pattern is called "sexual anorexia." This pattern is about avoidance. It can be very specific. Some people have certain sexual behaviors that they avoid. For some this pattern may mean that they avoid success, or eating, or spending. Spending, for example, reminds them of a fear of poverty or of not having money.*

4. Reactions	This is a broad category and refers to any way that your mind or your body tells you that you are afraid. You may have dreams that wake you up in the middle of the night. You might experience "flashbacks," or sudden memories that suddenly leap into your mind. Your body may develop aches and pains that don't seem related to any medical condition. Stomachaches, backaches and headaches are examples. Some chronic pain conditions, like fibromyalgia, could also point to a chronic fear of harm. Any stress related symptoms could fit into this category.
5. Repetition	This means that a person might seek to repeat experiences of trauma for two primary reasons. First, he might hope for a different result. This pattern leads to statements like, "why do you keep beating your head against the wall?" Why do some people seem to keep going back to damaging relationships or situations? Second, a person might repeat a traumatic situation, this time trying to be the one who is in the power position, the one who is creating the harm. There is the mistaken notion that by doing this, the pain of earlier memories will be diminished. This is sometimes referred to as the "victim to victimizer" cycle and is often behind any kind of offending behavior.
6. Bonds	This pattern describes finding others who will help you play out old situations. When this person "bonds" they get into relationships with people who remind them in some way of the person or persons who created the original harm. Why do our spouses sometimes remind us of characteristics of our mothers or our fathers? Examine any of your relationships in life and ask if you are not seeking to replay old patterns with this person for either of the reasons described in no. 5. In the cartoon strip "Peanuts," for example, why does Charlie Brown keep going back to a rather spiteful Lucy, the one who always pulls the football away?
7. Pleasure	This is one of the most painful patterns, possibly literally. People who have this pattern find pleasure in pain. Those who get involved with sado-masochistic behavior, for example, find sexual high from painful situations. The so-called "pleasure" received within the pain is an illusion of intimacy and love. It could be that they are recreating situations from their past, ones in which they found the only touch or attention they received. It could also mean

	that the excitement and adrenaline or the fear and danger involved get neuro-chemically programmed in their heads.
8. Shame	*Old wounds create the core belief that "I am a bad and worthless person." These people wouldn't know how to be happy or content. They find a sense of identity from feeling shameful. They can often play the victim or martyr role.*

> ***Take note in your journal which ones apply to you: As you read through these, write down any that seem familiar to you.***

Don't be frightened by them. Knowing what you know can help you and your group, or you and your therapist, create new behaviors and boundaries that will help break the pattern.

The final segment of Assignment Three is really the scariest but possibly the most helpful. Working on it has the best potential for interrupting your sex addiction cycle. It involves understanding your fantasies.

First, a principle:

> **Fantasies are an attempt to create an ideal world or scenario in which all of our wounds are healed.**

Think about it. Fantasies are the way in which we correct pain from our past. This doesn't have to be pain about sex. *It is pain about who we really are.* Fantasies may correct our sense of who we are. In our fantasies we are powerful, successful and loveable. In our fantasies we get touched, praised, nurtured and affirmed. We are immensely desirable.

Take athletic fantasies for example. Don't many of us have those? In them we find athletic greatness. We are stars and receive adulation. I have many basketball fantasies in which I correct all the mistakes, the losses and the failures of the past.

What about money fantasies? In mine, I have all the money I need for anything. I might win the lottery and have houses, cars, boats and planes. People love me and want to be with me because I am so rich.

Now turn to sexual fantasies. What are you correcting? It may simply be that you aren't getting enough sex, at least in your own mind. You need to be desired and affirmed. You need to be touched. You need to feel like you are admired and affirmed. Everybody wants you and would just die to be with you and would do anything for you.

It may be more complicated than that. Before we go any further, do this exercise. Be careful. I am going to ask you to describe your most common fantasy. Try not to get into it too far. Be an observer of it, not a participant. Answer the following four questions about what seems to you to be the fantasy that you are the most likely to play out in your mind. It may be the most recent. It may be the one that you have played out a thousand or more times over the course of your life. It may have variations. The people may have changed. Distill out the **theme**. Don't be graphic. Don't write the great American pornography novel.

In your fantasy:

Who shows up? What do they look like? Are they male or female? Does it involve one person or more than one? Is he or she tall, short, fat, skinny, blonde, red head, or brunette and/or do they have other physical characteristics like large breasts, long legs (do you get the picture)?
What do they act like? What is his or her emotional nature? Are they kind, sympathetic and compassionate? Do they act seductive? Do they seem to intensely want you? What is their personality?
Where does it take place? What is the setting, the mood and the ambience? Is it on a mountaintop, in the bedroom or in front of a fire?
What is the nature of the sexual activity? Be specific about it, but you don't need to be detailed. For example, sexual intercourse or oral sex is general but not graphic. Be fearless as you describe this.

Most of you will discover that perhaps only one of these four categories stands out to you. You may not care who shows up as long as a certain sexual activity takes place. You may not care about the sex so much as long as a certain kind of person is involved. What is important to you can be really crucial. Some would suggest that if sex is not important, for example, you may be more of a romance or love addict.

Be courageous. Be honest. Remember that your secrets have kept you in bondage. There is no sin that can separate you from the love of God.

In your journal, write a brief paragraph that describes the <u>themes</u> of your most common sexual fantasy.

Now, once you have the description of your most common fantasy, the main question is, what does it mean. Ask yourself what it suggests to you about your needs. Remember the principle; this fantasy could be your attempt to heal wounds.

We should not forget that there may be other reasons why you have this fantasy. It could be based on actual life experiences that were really exciting to you. It could be based on pornography that you have seen. It could be the result of the adrenaline that you have created in thinking it up. My guess is that even if these things are true, the fantasy speaks to the deepest longings of your heart for love and nurture.

Perhaps the person who shows up resembles a person who caused you to feel abandoned. Maybe she possesses the characteristics of love, nurture and desire that you long for. The setting could be one in which you feel safe, excited or stimulated. It might also be some kind of reenactment of previous experiences, even traumatic ones (remember the nature of traumatic reactions described above). The kind of sex you think about might symbolize to you ultimate excitement. It might also symbolize ultimate love. Fantasizing about oral sex, for example may suggest to you that you are either being completely accepted or that you are entirely consuming the essence of your sexual partner.

Why is this important? *If it is true that this fantasy is an attempt to heal a part of your soul, and you only seek to shut this fantasy off, it will quiet the voice of your soul.*

You must give voice to the deepest longings of your soul. If you don't it will find other ways to talk to you. It craves to be heard, perhaps just as you did when you were a child.

If you can hear that voice and find healthy ways to heal the wounds, your fantasies will go away. You won't need them.

Talk with your group about what are better answers to your needs for affirmation, praise, touch, nurture, safety and belonging.

As Christians, we know that the main answer is a relationship with God through his Son Jesus Christ. Then it is a relationship with other Christians. In your relationship with God you must come to understand that He loves you just as you are. There is no sin that stops Him from loving you. In your relationship with others you must find safety, affirmation, healthy touch and a true sense of belonging.

> *Ask God to teach you what your fantasy means and how you can find more ultimate fulfillment in a deepening relationship with Him. Journal about this and discuss it with your group and/or your therapist.*

Congratulations! You have just finished the most difficult emotional assignment in the entire workbook. If you have done it well, you will find that you have begun to find new freedom from old memories and thoughts.

Principle Two

We believe in God, accept the grace offered through His Son Jesus Christ, and surrender our lives and our wills to Him on a daily basis.

Assignment One - "Do You Want to Get Well?"

In the book of John, chapter 5, there is a great story of one of the healing miracles that Jesus performs. As the story goes, there is, outside of Jerusalem, a pool called Bethesda. Many lame, paralyzed and blind would lie there trying to find healing. The belief was that there was an angel who would come down and stir the water. The first one to get into the pool after this would be healed. There was a man who had been paralyzed for 38 years. Jesus comes across this scene. Stop for a moment. If this were you encountering this paralyzed man, what would you say or try to do? Perhaps something like, "That must be tough," or "How can I help you get into the pool?" You might be wondering to yourself, how did this happen, what is this man's condition or illness?

Jesus asks a rather interesting question: "Do you want to get well?" This sounds like a rather stupid question. Why wouldn't a man who has been lying by a healing pool for 38 years want to get well? Jesus is the master psychologist. The man answers, "Sir, I don't have anyone to help me into the pool and when I try someone else gets in my way."

By the nature of that response we, too, might wonder if he really wanted to get well. Your task in this assignment is to ask yourself the question, "Do I want to get well?" Let's be honest, the work that we are trying to teach you in this workbook is not rocket science. It is not difficult to understand, at least. Why is it so difficult to do?

> *In your journal write any reason that you can think of why you shouldn't give up your addiction. Don't be too pious saying that you can't think of any. Who has been in your way? What factors have kept you away from healing? Think about what you have said to yourself about why it is so hard to find healing.*

James, the brother of Christ, says that we can be guilty of being "double-minded." He says, "Come near to God and He will come near to you. Wash your hands, you sinners, and purify your hearts, you double-minded." (James 4:8) There is a part of you that has wanted to get well and a part of you that has not. Sex has been your most important need and, as such, a "friend." Sex has been what you thought about in your loneliest and most stressful times. Your sexual fantasies brought you "comfort," or so you thought. It is hard to think about being without them.

Begin to think that you may have to grieve to get well.

Make a list of what it will cost you to get well. Which behaviors will you have to give up? (Review your work in Assignment One of Principle One if you need to.) Which friends must you avoid because they encourage your sinfulness instead of your purity? Will you have to change jobs or clubs or activities or residences? How you dress or where you go for recreation? The way you interact with the opposite (or same) sex? What on-going consequences are you going to have to face without acting out more? Be specific in counting the cost. Outline what it will look like to surrender control to Christ.

Next, examine your feelings. Write the emotions you experience when you think about what it would be like to be free from your sexual sin. Sure, you probably feel some gladness, but probe deeper. You also may feel some fear or sadness or even anger. After all, your addiction has been your friend for a long time. You wonder who and how you will be without it. Confess to God all your feelings, the "bad" ones as well as the "acceptable" ones. Admit honestly to Him the parts of your spirit that may resist surrendering your addiction and your control over your life.

Perhaps you're feeling ashamed or even hopeless after examining your acting out behaviors and the consequences you've experienced. You've remembered your earlier attempts to achieve sexual purity, and you wonder how this time can be different. What's going to make this effort succeed?

Your work in Assignment One of the first Principle has highlighted your powerlessness over the sexual sin in your life, and you see the depth of your bondage. Maybe you're more afraid than you've ever been. It's beginning to dawn on you that God, also, is aware of your sins. He knows the depravity of your thoughts and actions. How could there possibly be any hope for one like you?

This central question brings us to the heart of Principle Two. It is, indeed, a heart question, as you seek to repair (or perhaps to create for the first time) your relationship with God. Can you trust Him with your heart? Can you believe in the grace of His Son to be sufficient to cover all your sins? You're convinced your sin matters to God, but does your pain matter, too?

Despite our claim to be a Christian, when we're totally honest, most of us don't fully trust God. Many of us hardly trust Him. Some of us do not trust Him at all. You know you believe in God. That's not the question. The problem isn't belief; it's faith. Do you trust that God will be enough for you--period? That's the core question of Principle Two.

You may feel ashamed of this lack of faith in God. It may be one of your hidden secrets, along with the ones you admitted in your work of Principle One. You don't understand how you can distrust God, because you've been involved with religious things most (or all) of your life.

The answer probably lies in the explanation of spiritual abuse. You may want to review the section in *Faithful and True* for a reminder of what it means to have been spiritually abused. Briefly, spiritual abuse occurs when someone uses the Bible or a position of spiritual authority more as a weapon than as a guide. It's when others attempt to motivate you into right actions by fear or shame, instead of by encouraging you into a loving relationship with God. Spiritual abuse also happens when you experience any other kind of abuse (physical, emotional or sexual) at the hands of someone who is a spiritual figure in your life. This means that if you were abused by a pastor, youth leader or someone in a similar role, you're automatically a victim of spiritual abuse.

Like other forms of abuse, spiritual abuse warps our view of God and of others. We naturally form our view of God according to our experiences with our earthly parents, especially our fathers. If your dad was physically or sexually abusive, how can you believe God wants the best for you? If a spiritual authority figure was harsh and judgmental, how can you understand grace? How can you trust God to meet your needs and to love you unconditionally if you haven't known safe people who loved you, no matter what you did?

Write a description of your view of God. What is God like in your mind? What are some words that describe Him? (If you'd prefer, draw a picture of how you see God.) Remember, the way you write or how well you draw doesn't matter. Don't worry about grammar. What's important is that you clearly identify what you really believe about God.

Most people who struggle with their sexual behavior feel terribly alone. You're isolated and desperately lonely. You feel alienated from God and others. Yes, the secret of your sexual sin keeps you from real intimacy with others, but the issue probably goes far beyond your problem with addiction. Your history of feeling isolated and alone probably dates back long before you started acting out. It probably began in your family. It comes from the core wounds of abandonment.

A thorough explanation of what it means to have been abandoned is found in primary sources like *Faithful and True* or the *Faithful and True Workbook*. I also give a brief description in this workbook in Assignment Three of Principle One. Review some of these materials if necessary.

For our purpose here, remember that we're abandoned when some of our fundamental needs for physical, emotional, sexual or spiritual nurture haven't been met by our caregivers. As I outlined spiritual abuse in the last section, if a key spiritual figure in your life wasn't available in some way (physically or emotionally), then you've suffered spiritual abandonment. Again, that experience will color your view of God. You'll have difficulty believing God is really concerned about you.

List the people you feel abandoned you in some critical way. Describe the abandonment.

_____   _____
_____   _____
_____   _____
_____   _____
_____   _____
_____   _____

Find five Scriptures that describe God's care and concern for you. Write down the references. Read them daily for the next week.

_____
_____
_____
_____
_____

Assignment Two - The Choice I've Never Made

You may be feeling defensive after reading the title of this assignment: "The choice I've never made." Maybe you bristle at the implication you haven't tried to do something about your addiction. You've probably done a lot of things about your addiction – except become sober from it.

Most of our attempts to deal with our addiction are unsuccessful because they're more about controlling behavior or lust instead of surrendering it. We use a variety of excuses to rationalize this approach. *(Review Assignment Two of Principle One, which outlines several examples of this kind of "stinking thinking.")* We also excuse half-hearted attempts to surrender with rationalizations like "I don't want to make radical changes like ending a 'friendship' because that might embarrass my family when people question why;" or "God knows I need to support myself financially, so it's understandable that I can't quit traveling for my job."

In more subtle ways we sometimes try to control or bargain with God about our addiction. We make attempts to stop acting out, and bargain that God will do something for us in exchange. Many of you have heard my story about surrendering my use of pornography in exchange for God making me a tennis star. At age 16 at a Fellowship of Christian Athletes camp, I dedicated myself to ministry and vowed to stop stealing *Playboy*. In my spiritual immaturity, I believed God would reward me with tennis success. I fantasized about winning Wimbledon and witnessing to the Queen. If you had asked me, I'd have assured you I'd tried to surrender my habit to God. What I'd really done was attempt to manipulate God into giving me something I deeply wanted: to be an outstanding tennis player.

Most of us have made many of these surrogate surrenders. We're usually quick to "surrender" when we're facing tough consequences of our addiction. We're afraid our partner is pregnant, so we promise to stop the affair if God will only spare us the complication of pregnancy. Or we try to get by with a partial surrender. We give up an acting out behavior that we think is especially bad, but we hold on to other, supposedly less offensive, behaviors. We end an affair, but we continue to use pornography or masturbate. That approach is really only substituting one sin for another. That exchange hardly constitutes genuine surrender! Sometimes we may even stop acting out totally for a while (by "white knuckling"), but we don't truly surrender our hearts and wills to God.

Some of us have tried to manipulate and control others, especially our spouses, by pseudo efforts to surrender. We may stop acting out with other people, but instead we bug our spouse excessively for sex. We may agree to go to counseling as long as our mate agrees to stop pestering us about it. But though we sit in a counselor's office for an hour a week, we never commit to a genuine process of change.

Occasionally, an addict will surrender the specifics of his sexual addiction, but will continue to hold on to his heart. By that I mean that the now-sober addict will refuse to look any deeper than the sinful behaviors. If he's not physically acting out, he considers himself cured. He won't look at his character defects of pride or jealousy or insecurity or control. He's really nothing more than what AA calls a "dry drunk." Usually, he's still medicating with other, more acceptable means, like working or spending.

That kind of "surrender" falls far short of God's call. He challenges us to "offer your bodies as living sacrifices, holy and pleasing to God – this is your spiritual act of worship. Do not conform any longer to the pattern of this world, but be transformed by the renewing of your mind" (Rom. 12: 1). God is much more concerned with our transformation than with our mere sobriety. Can you honestly say you've truly surrendered to God in a spiritual sense? Are you willing to allow Him to transform you and mold you into the person He wants you to be?

A final example of a false kind of "choice" we make to surrender is our attempt to do it on our own. Because of our shame and our fear of being known, we're tempted to try to recover without involving anyone else in our process. We believe we can recover in isolation by simply reading books, completing workbook exercises or maybe talking with a therapist. But we won't share with other men individually, and we sure won't go to a group where others are seeking to become faithful and true.

This persistence of seeking recovery without becoming vulnerable to others exposes a key stronghold in many addicts' lives: the belief "I can do this on my own!" We trust our ability to help ourselves more than we trust God. We hope that if we just try long enough, hard enough or "right" enough, we'll be successful. Instead of admitting powerlessness and surrendering totally to God, we try to work harder at getting it right by ourselves. Such efforts are doomed to fail. (I'll talk more in a later Principle about the pitfalls of refusing to be in accountability and fellowship with others.)

What are some of your excuses for not surrendering your addiction totally to God?

List some of the bargains or deals you've made with God about your acting out.

How have you tried to control or manipulate others by promising to get sober from your addiction?

In what practical ways have you declared, "I can do this!" instead of relying on God? Describe any attempts you've made to achieve sobriety by yourself. Describe the results.

Assignment Three - The Hope I Must Embrace

I invite you to do an imaginative exercise somewhat like you did when you considered your most frequent sexual fantasy. This time, though, you'll be imagining a scene that springs from hope, instead of one that comes from the pain of the past. First, if your description or picture of God (Assignment Two of this Principle) is of an angry or distant Being, recreate (at least in your mind) an image that more accurately portrays God's love and grace.

Now, I want you to see yourself interacting with that kind of God. This is the "Abba" God – the intimate "daddy" God. This is the God who would ride you on His shoulders, throw ball with you, listen to your stories and comfort your fears. This is the perfect father. (A good description of this Biblical view of God may be found in Sandra Wilson's *Into Abba's Arms* or in many of the writings by Max Lucado.)

Imagine the two of you talking and laughing together. Try to picture some specific activity or conversation. Observe all the details of the setting. Let this scene become real in your mind.

You can be confident that God is truly the loving, caring Abba Father you imagined. It's safe to depend on Him, because He is 100% trustworthy. To surrender to God is to place your life and will into the care of One who is eager to be in relationship with you. God loved you enough that He sent His only Son to die on the cross for your sins.

The connection you've sought through sinful sexual practices is really the longing for intimacy with God. Your passion is to be known and loved and cherished, despite your faults. Only God can fulfill that desire. Intimacy with Him can never be found through pursuits of the flesh.

An important part of your transformation process will be to experience the fathering of your Abba God. Only His love and the grace of Christ can sustain and heal you. All other substitutes are false. And the path to this intimacy with God begins with surrender.

Write a description of this encounter with God in your journal. Be specific; include as much detail as possible. What did you do? How did God respond? What did you say to each other? Share your image with someone from your L.I.F.E. group.

Compose a statement of surrender to God. (The Third Step Prayer of AA is an example.) Remember, the wording and grammar aren't important. The intent of your heart is what matters. Offer the prayer at your next group meeting or share it with your pastor or accountability partner.

Principle Three

We will courageously make a list of all of our sins and weaknesses and will confess those to a person of spiritual authority.

Assignment One - Admitting Our Darkness

Principle Three challenges you to understand your sinful nature. We are all sinners and fall short of the glory of God, according to Paul. We are inheritors of original sin, the sin of pride. We have thought that we could control our own life and that we could find solutions to our deepest problems. In Principle Two we remember that only God can restore our lives if we surrender to Him. Working on Principle Three will be painful, just as Principle One was. It is supposed to be. Pain is not a bad thing if it reminds us of how far from God we are. It teaches us to let go of control. Don't be afraid of the pain.

Remember that we seek to understand our sinfulness, not so that we can increase our shame, but so that we can learn to depend more on God.

In assignment one, we want to know how you have lied to yourself and to others. Alcoholics Anonymous has many great phrases. Two of them are "Stinking Thinking" and "Your own best thinking is what got you here." Clinicians might say that we have "distorted cognitive thinking." Schools of secular and Christian counseling might seek to have us heal through changing our thoughts. As Christians, we want to take every thought captive to Christ. Stinking Thinking includes all the lies that we have believed.

The fact is we have thought we could heal ourselves and that we could lie our way out of all situations. The truth is that we are afraid of getting help and of getting honest about who we really are. I believe that we suffer from **Intimacy Disorder**. This means that we believe that we are bad and worthless people and that no one will take care of us. We also think that if anyone really knew us, they would hate us and leave us.

It has been said that all addicts are chronic liars. They seek to constantly manipulate the opinion of others. They avoid the truth. They fear getting caught. They have anxiety about consequences. They may even be arrogant and think that they can get away with their lies.

The first part of understanding the lies that we have told is to understand the lies that we have told ourselves. That is part of our original sin nature. When the serpent tempted Eve, he told the first lie. It was that she could eat the apple and that she wouldn't die. Telling lies to ourselves is a lot like that. We believe that we can get away with something and that it won't hurt us to do so. We believe that we won't get caught and that what we are doing isn't hurting us or anyone else.

Did you ever tell yourself that your sexual sins wouldn't hurt anyone? Did you ever tell yourself that you wouldn't hurt yourself? It's a lot like eating too much food and believing that we won't get fat, drinking too much alcohol and believing that we won't harm our bodies, or that we can ignore our health and not get sick.

Did you ever convince yourself that you wouldn't get caught? Did you think that you were being so careful and discreet? What precautions have you ever taken not to be caught? What manipulations have you done to avoid getting caught?

Did you ever tell yourself that your sins weren't that bad? Did you ever justify a lesser sexual sin because it prevented you from doing a more serious one? Did you ever say that you had the power to quit when you really wanted to? Did you ever believe that your sins weren't all that deadly? For example, have you ever said that as long as your sins were never discovered, no one would get hurt?

> *Write in your journal about any lies that you have told yourself about your sexual sins.*

Think back over the years of your life. Do you remember the first lie that you ever told to cover up sinful behavior? How old were you? Who did you tell it to? Did you get away with it? Write down your answers in your journal.

> *Do you remember the first lie that you told to cover up a sexually sinful behavior? Ask yourself the same questions as immediately above. Write down these answers in your journal.*
>
> *If you can, trace the history of your deceitful behavior since that time. Make a list in your journal of all the major lies you have told in your life.*
>
> *What is your most recent lie? What was that about? Who did you tell that to? Are you still keeping it secret?*

When we experience Intimacy Disorder, it is hardest to tell the truth to those that we love the most. One way of saying it is that the person we are most afraid of losing will be the one we have the hardest time telling the truth to.

You may be experiencing this dynamic in your group. It may have been relatively easy to come into your L.I.F.E. group and get honest. You're finding it impossible, however, to tell the truth to somebody you really love.

Write down the specific name of those people that you are the most afraid of finding out the truth about yourself, particularly your sexual sins. Next to each one of these names, write what you are the most afraid of. Obviously, your wife will show up as the most important person on this list. How much have you been worrying about her reaction to the truth of your behaviors?

Name   **What You Are Most Afraid Of**

_____
_____
_____
_____
_____

Now ask yourself if you are willing to go through life worrying about these kinds of consequences. Part of your program in L.I.F.E. Ministries to become faithful and true will be to build a character of honesty. It will no longer be comfortable for you to live with your lies and deceptions. You will long for a character of integrity. Even now in your recovery start thinking about the courage it will take to start getting honest with the people around you that you love the most.

One of the great principles of becoming faithful and true is accepting the risk when we start telling the truth.

I like to think about risk as one practical way we surrender our lives to Christ. We can't control our lives. If we accept that only God can, then what risks are we able to take? Other people's reactions, including our wives', are in the hands of God. Can you also surrender reactions to Christ?

> *Write your thoughts and feelings about this in your journal. Pray for courage to start getting honest.*

Assignment Two - Exposing Our Darkness

At this point in your program, you are waking up from the fog of your acting out behaviors. You are starting to get honest. Reality is sinking in. This might be frightening and discouraging. You were hoping for what AA calls, "a softer, gentler way." Be aware of your own distorted thinking. Satan is also talking to you right now saying something like, "If this healing journey is so great, why do you feel so bad?"

Have you ever had some injury or some kind of surgery? You know that the recovery process is often painful. You may feel a lot worse before you start feeling better. Healing from sexual sin and addiction is no different.

Now, it is time to really get honest about your life. When Jesus confronted a man who had been possessed by demons, He asked him, "What is your name?" The man said, "My name is Legion." It may seem to you that the sins of your life are Legion and you may be overwhelmed by the enormity of it.

Be aware that you are entering a stage of grieving — grieving all the painful experiences of the past. You will be dealing with your shame and asking yourself the questions, "How could I have done these terrible things?" This is all normal. What we are after now is exposing all of this to the light. You have been hiding your life for years and your silence has been killing you. It is time to expose it to the healing power of God's grace.

It is perhaps easiest to divide your life into stages and categories. As you look at the various areas of sin in your life, remember the words of Paul when he wrote about not doing the things he wanted to and about doing the things he didn't want to. There are sins of commission and sins of omission. Think not only about the sins you've done, but also about the good that you haven't done. Don't forget to include your actions or lack of actions, and your negative or sinful thoughts and lack of positive ones.

Divide your life up into stages. One simple division would be childhood, adolescence, teenage, young adult, mid-life and senior years (Obviously, some of you have not reached all of these stages).

Next, think about categories of your life. such as your family, your education, your social relationships, your job or vocation, your sexuality and your spiritual life.

You may be overwhelmed by a large variety or complexity of thoughts. Keep it simple. Start journaling about one age and one category and then move on to another. Like all of the assignments in this workbook, this is not a one-time exercise. You should add thoughts and memories as long as they keep coming up.

For the purpose of Living in Freedom Everyday sexually, let's use sex as the category to begin with. The first questions you would ask yourself are, "When was the first time you remember having an inappropriate thought or behavior about sex? How old were you? Where did it happen and what were the consequences, if any?" Then grow yourself up and go year by year. One purpose of doing this is that you will probably see how your sexual addiction developed over time.

You may fill pages and pages of information. This is a long assignment. Don't worry about it. The first time that you work through it, you may only hit the basics. You can go back and get more detailed later. Remember that you are practicing getting honest and you are taking many risks.

Add categories as you are able. There may be many other things that you have lied about or crazy behaviors that you have done. In my story, for example, the first time that I looked at pornography, I stole the magazine. I was both a sexual sinner and a thief. Did you ever cheat on a test, skip a class or tell a lie to gain approval from others?

As you work on this assignment, I want you to take frequent breaks. Talk to someone and get some support and encouragement. Remember again, we *all* sin and fall short of the glory of God. If we didn't, we wouldn't need Jesus.

A final word of caution: this is not an exercise in which you discover in a grandiose way what a terrific sinner you are. In my early days of recovery I used to go to AA meetings because there were no sex addict meetings. There were times in these groups when someone would tell his story of acting out with alcohol. There were those who I often felt seemed to like telling how bad it got. It was as if they were bragging about how terrible they were so that the fact that they were currently sober would seem all the more amazing. Let me assure you that there will always be someone who can top your story or who has committed more depraved sins than you.

When you are sharing about your assignment in groups there is another word of caution. Don't be graphic in describing your sexual behaviors. There are times when you will just be triggering other members of the group. There may also be times when you are educating group members about other forms of sexual acting out.

Assignment Three - Confessing Our Darkness

This assignment is quite simple but extremely vital to your spiritual recovery. In James 5:16, the brother of Jesus tells us that we should confess our sins to one another. This is your time to do so in a formal way. By "formal" I mean in a way that is spiritually significant to you.

You have taken note that this is assignment three of Principle Three. This workbook hasn't asked you to do confession sooner because we wanted you to carefully consider your life. We also didn't want you rushing out confessing to everyone who came along. There is a temptation for some to do this. These people have a feeling that if they confess and get it over with everything will be right with their worlds. This can feel cathartic and may be dangerous. We don't want you confessing to everyone.

Here are several questions to ask yourself as you prepare for this assignment:

1. *Have you done serious and prayerful work on the first two assignments?*
2. *Have you looked at all areas of your life, not just the sexual ones?*
3. *What is your reason for confessing at this time? What do you hope to get out of it? Do you hope to be instantly forgiven by everyone? Do you hope to be done with this process forever?*

I remember a famous evangelist who years ago publicly confessed his sexual sins on his TV show. He cried and lamented. Then he quoted a variety of scriptures about God's grace and how we all need to forgive each other. There was something about his sincerity and humility that didn't feel quite right. Several months later he relapsed with the same sexual behaviors.

Here are some points I think of:

Confession is done out of humility, not arrogance.

Don't confess to anyone whose forgiveness you might be trying to manipulate.

Don't confess if you expect that this is the one and only time.

Don't confess if you're just trying to get it over with.

Don't confess if you're thinking that others will be mad at you if you don't.

Confession is a genuine act of repentance, not something you do because you got caught.

I would encourage you to consider all of this and do some praying and reflecting about it. Then get some feedback from your L.I.F.E. group about your motivation and readiness to confess at this time.

As you can tell, I have a lot of feelings about confession. I have always been bothered by the brief and usually collective acts of confession that most of us have done at church throughout our lives. We might print something in the bulletin that we read together. We might be instructed to pray silently to God about our sins. That's not enough.

The Roman Catholics have been better at this. I have many friends among them and I'm aware of how perfunctory or ritualistic confession may have become for many of them. It is, however, a sacrament, a *sacred* act to be done with a person, a priest, of spiritual authority. Let's consider that principle to be important.

Your next part of this assignment is to consider who is a spiritual authority for you. I want you to be careful here and don't just automatically assume that it is your current pastor. Maybe you don't have a current pastor because you don't have a regular church relationship. Maybe you don't like your current pastor.

Here are some more things to think about. Start with the religious traditions of your youth. Even though some of you may have converted to a more evangelical or some different church, you may still have places in your childhood heart that recognize the spiritual authority of your youth. I have talked to many people, for example, who have converted from Roman Catholicism to a Protestant denomination. There are still parts of them that remember the spiritual authority of a priest. Being honest, you may reject that authority today, but I'm asking you to examine your heart. What is it telling you?

Part of your thinking should consider the role of authority in the Church. Do you believe that God calls some to be pastors and evangelists and that they have been given spiritual authority to represent God's grace? Today, who do you say is "my pastor?"

Maybe it's still someone from the past. Possible candidates would be the person who led you to the Lord, a person who discipled or mentored you, a previous pastor who is no longer at your current church or is at some other church, or a respected Bible teacher or Sunday School teacher. It might even be a Christian counselor or possibly the leader of your L.I.F.E. group.

Write the name of that person who most represents spiritual authority to you.

_____

Now, is it possible to schedule an appointment with that person to go over all the work you've been doing in Principle Three? I have known these appointments to sometimes take hours because there is a lot to say.

If it is possible, make that appointment and write down the time in your journal. You will then be reporting this to your L.I.F.E. group, which will be holding you accountable to do it. If it is not possible with the first person on your list, keep going until you find a person who is available. It could be someone that you don't know yet. I'll be honest with you, the first time I confessed my whole sexual story, it was to a retired Roman Catholic priest who was the chaplain at the treatment center where I was a patient. I didn't know him from Adam, but he was a person of spiritual authority to me that day. He was the first person to hear the story in its entirety. When he said God forgives you, I believed him. That is the kind of experience that I long for with all of you.

Now, when you have had this time of confession, I want you to take some time and journal what it was like. It may just be a few sentences or paragraphs. It may be longer, but it should be a definite entry in your journal. When you have done this, use some group time during check in to report on what this was like. You might also, at some point, agree to be the person who does the talk on Principle Three for that night. This will be wonderful experience for you to share.

Need I remind you again that God loves you and sent His Son to die for just those sins that you have written about in your journal. I pray that you will simply find one person who will be the human ears and voice that will remind you of that.

Principle Four

We seek accountability and to build our character as children of God

Assignment One - Accepting Accountability

The first time you work through this assignment, you have one main job. That is to find a **sponsor.** As you participate in your L.I.F.E. group, you will see that the final chapter in this workbook is a blueprint from the book of Nehemiah about accountability. You may want to review that material as you begin working on this Principle, and even discuss one or more of the Nehemiah Principles at future meetings. Principle Four is about accountability and about character. You will find in the early days of learning about accountability that you have probably had many incorrect notions of what it means. You may have had many thoughts of what it should be. You may even have had one accountability partner. That is not bad, but it hasn't fully worked. In this assignment we want you to start thinking of that partner as the one main guide who directs your program.

You are too smart, however, and too skillful at deceit to let only one person truly know you. It will take more than one to keep you honest and directed in the early days. So, as AA says, "First things first." You need a sponsor. Below is a checklist about sponsorship, which you need to study in order to begin your understanding of what we mean.

Sponsors

And the things you have heard me say in the presence of many witnesses entrust to reliable men who will also be qualified to teach others. 2 Timothy 2:2 (NIV)

Below are some characteristics of a sponsor. Check the ones that appeal to you as something that you need.

_____A sponsor is someone who will hold you accountable. You will be able to share with this person all of your past sexual sins, your acting out behaviors, your rituals and your fantasies. You will develop a plan for staying sober with your sponsor. If he ever sees you coming close to doing any of these behaviors, he will directly confront you about them in love.

_____A sponsor is someone who will give you encouragement. As you slowly make progress, a sponsor will celebrate with you your success.

_____A sponsor is someone who you can talk to and who will listen. Whenever you feel tempted, lonely, frightened, sad or angry, you can call a sponsor to talk things over. Sometimes he will meet with you during such emergencies until the crisis passes.

_____A sponsor is someone with whom you can pray. The two of you can seek the Lord's guidance together. You may also share Bible study.

_____A sponsor is a model. Ideally, he should be someone who has had at least one year of successful sobriety from his addictions. His success should serve as an inspiration to you. Some groups will be so new that there won't be men in them with this length of time. Sponsors don't always need to be coming out of sexual addiction. My first sponsor was a man who had 10 years of sobriety from alcohol. He knew how to model accountability. What I'm saying is that some L.I.F.E. groups may need to rely on finding sponsors in places other than the group itself.

_____A sponsor is a guide. He will teach you about tools to use in recovery and show you the path to take to be successful. He will go over your assignments as you do them. He can direct your reading outside of the group. He may have ideas about therapy or spiritual direction. He is the General.

The following table summarizes the roles of both the Sponsor and the Group Member in the sponsoring relationship. You can use it to help identify, recruit and set expectations with your sponsor.

Sponsor Responsibilities	Group Member Responsibilities
Must be willing to confront with boundaries and consequences	Must be willing to submit to authority
Encourage the member with positive affirmations	Must be willing to sign a contract/plan with top and bottom lines (see example)
Must have a plan/contract submitted by the member	
Be a good listener (don't try to fix)	
Must be available	
Be willing to lead in prayer and teach member to pray	Be willing to pray on the phone and in person
Meet physically with the member at least once a week and check the workbook assignments	Show the sponsor the workbook assignments
Call the member if he does not call by a set time	Call the sponsor by a set time determined by the two of you
Strongly recommend a counselor	Get a counselor if financially able
Ask the group member to state feelings	State feelings (use a feelings chart if necessary)
Ask if there are any lustful thoughts or temptations	State honestly what the struggles of the day are
Ask if the member is taking care of himself in exercise and diet	Get enough rest and exercise and eat a healthy diet

What do you look for in a sponsor? It cannot be the spouse. It cannot be a member of the opposite sex. It should be someone you can relate to and preferably someone who is a recovering sex addict with more sobriety than yourself. Some suggestions include:

-a relative
-a friend
-a pastor
-someone in the church
-someone with AA or SA experience
-another member of the group with similar sobriety

Keep in mind that sponsorship is based on re-parenting and this person will in many ways be like a surrogate parent. A sponsor must be tough, wise and loving all in the same role. If you were abandoned emotionally, physically or spiritually by one of your parents, having a sponsor may seem very strange. There may be times when you don't you're your sponsor, and that's OK. He is like a signpost, showing you the way. There are times that I don't like the speed limit signs on the road when I am in a hurry. There will be times when you don't like what your sponsor is telling you. Addicts, after all, love to isolate and not be responsible to anyone else. On the other hand, you may also find a wonderful presence in a sponsor that you have never found before. The surrogate parent part of the sponsor's role can help heal some of your wounds from the past.

Is there anyone in your life right now who would be a candidate for being a sponsor? If you don't know anyone, your group may give you someone who has volunteered to be a sponsor until you find a more permanent one. If you do know someone, be sure to ask him if he is able to make such a commitment.

You will need to meet with your sponsor at least once a week outside of group time. You will probably need to call him at least once every day during the first few weeks of your recovery. The next three pages contain a sample "Sponsor Contract" you might use to formalize the commitments you and your sponsor are making, along with some sample questions and other criteria to help both of you understand and remain accountable to those commitments. Those pages are followed by some comprehensive material on the benefits of a ninety-day period of abstinence from sexual activity.

> *Write down the name of your sponsor:* _____

> *In your journal, keep a log of the times you have met and the times you have called. Keep this separate from your other work. You can refer to it as a way of knowing how well you are doing at staying connected.*

Sponsor Contract

Sponsor Name: _____ Phone Number: _____

Group Leader Name: _____ Phone Number: _____

Member Leader: _____ Phone Number: _____

Address: _____ City, State, Zip _____

Age: ___ Occupation: _____ Work Phone: _____

Spouses Name: _____ Married How Long: _____

Children: _____ Step Children: _____

Currently attending church: [__] Yes [__] No. Where: _____

Are you now or have you in the past, worked with a counselor/therapist? [__] Yes [__] No

If yes, when and for how long? _____

Have you ever been involved in a recovery ministry before? [__] Yes [__] No

If yes, which program(s): _____

Is there anything else that I as your sponsor should know about you?

Other accountability partners (names and phone numbers):

1._____

2._____

3._____

4._____

5._____

Calling time(s): M_____ T_____ W_____Th_____ F_____ Sa_____ Su_____

Suggestions for Top and Bottom Lines

Defining Bottom Lines

Think about what you need to do to avoid situations that tempt you in behaviors such as the following:

objectify
fantasize
masturbate
control others
control self
compulsively watch TV
compulsively exercise
compulsively eat
engage in sexual sin with others
compulsively play video games
(especially those with inappropriate images)

Defining Top Lines

Think about what you need to do to make healthier choices in such areas as the following:

connect with safe people
exercise/care for your body
eat well
rest
play
daily recovery literature
prayer
Bible reading

****

My Top Lines:

1. _____
2. _____
3. _____
4. _____
5. _____

My Bottom Lines:

1. _____
2. _____
3. _____
4. _____
5. _____

Signature: _____ Date: _____

Witness: _____ Date: _____
(one witness should be your spouse, if married)

Witness: _____ Date: _____

Suggested Accountability Questions:

Feelings Check

How are you feeling?
What are you feeling?

Get Current

What's going on?
What happened today?

Accountability

Did you engage in any medicating behaviors today?
Did you objectify anyone today?
Did you fantasize?
Have you masturbated?
Have you been on any inappropriate Internet sites?
How much TV have you watched?
Have you taken care of yourself physically?
Has there been any provocative behavior? Voyeurism?
Are there any specific areas where you need accountability?
Have you fully disclosed everything you need to?

Ninety Days of Abstinence

For all of you who wish to recover from sexual sin and who are married, I recommend that you mutually commit to a temporary period of total abstinence. This commitment means no sex with yourself or with your spouse. Abstinence could be for any period of time, but I recommend 90 days.

I recommend abstinence for three reasons. First, by abstaining from genital sex you will experience a cleansing of your brain chemistry. An alcoholic needs to be sober for a number of days before the alcohol is completely out of his or her system. The same principle applies to those recovering from sexual addiction. Even fantasies produce chemicals in the brain that cause us to feel pleasure. These chemical reactions are a natural part of life. Sex addicts, however, have used this chemical reaction to medicate and escape their feelings. Ceasing all sexual activity can allow the brain chemistry to return to normal.

The second benefit of abstinence deals with the addictive characteristic called tolerance. Tolerance means the addict requires more of the addictive agent to achieve the same ends. An alcoholic, for example, develops tolerance so he or she requires more alcohol to become intoxicated. You may have built up a tolerance for sexual activity. You may find that you need a greater amount of sexual stimuli than you once did. This may have led you into more frequent sexual activity or more dangerous sex. This may also have affected your ability to experience sexual pleasure with your wife. The need for more and more may even have created impotence. Being abstinent for a period of time will help to reverse these symptoms. If you can complete the abstinence period, you will find that the joy of sex with your wife may return. If it has not, you may have to seek more specialized counseling.

A third reason I recommend abstinence deals with changing your core beliefs. Addicts hold the core belief that sex is their most important need. A period of abstinence reverses this belief and gradually teaches that sex is not your most important need; you can get along just fine without it.

A period of abstinence will help you deal with another false core belief that sex is equal to love. When you abstain from sex and still receive love from your wife, that continuing love challenges the core belief. If you are single, through abstinence you will learn that you can experience love from more intimate friendships than when you were sexually acting out.

The most obvious advantage of an abstinence contract for your marriage is that it takes the pressure of sex off your relationship and allows the two of you to begin building your relationship on a spiritual and emotional basis. For many couples, marital sex has been full of conflicts, arguments, and possibly even emotional pain. A period of abstinence allows you to begin to heal from some of this pain.

"Do not deprive each other except by mutual consent and for a time, so that you may devote yourselves to prayer. Then come together again so that Satan will not tempt you because of your lack of self-control". -1 Corinthians 7:5

During a time of abstinence intense feelings may surface; feelings you have kept bottled up for years. The period of abstinence will allow you an opportunity to deal with and heal from these feelings.

A bonus reason for abstinence has to do with the reason Paul suggested abstinence in 1 Corinthians 7:5. Abstaining from sexual activity allows a couple to devote themselves to prayer and spiritual renewal. Time spent with God reminds us that our love relationship with God is our most important relationship and deserves first place in our lives.

Which of these reasons for abstinence could be an advantage to your marriage? Abstinence must be a mutual agreement. Discuss the contract with your spouse. In my experience, spouses divide into two basic categories:
   • Some spouses welcome a period of sexual abstinence. Sex has been emotionally painful for years. Perhaps too many demands have been placed on them, or the sexual activity has been unpleasant. Whatever the case, a period of no sex will be a welcome relief.
   • Some spouses, however, fear abstinence. These spouses feel they need the assurance of a sexual relationship. They worry that their sexually-addicted spouses will continue to act out if sex is not present in their relationship. They may suffer from the belief that if they were more attractive or sexually willing, their spouses wouldn't have a problem. This belief is not true. I have known sex addicts married to beauty contest winners. Beauty and sexual willingness are not related to the spouse's sexual sin. The abstinence contract is important for such couples. It teaches them that the basis of their marital relationship should be spiritual and emotional, not sexual.

A married couple should not attempt a period of abstinence if they do not also have a plan for working on their relationship in other ways. This might include seeing a counselor or a variety of other strategies for developing healthy intimacy in a relationship without relying on sex.   There are many available resources for marriage enrichment which could significantly bless your marriage.

The above material is based on coverage of the same subject in the Faithful and True Workbook, which was mentioned in the Introduction. [ii]

Other aspects of a ninety day period of abstinence include the following:

No internet for 90 days, unless necessary for work.
If the Internet has been a part of your addictive behavior, disconnect and lock up the computer for 90 days (if the wife needs it she can have the key).   If the Internet is necessary for your work, discuss with your sponsor ways to avoid temptation.   We suggest one of the filter or accountability reporting programs.

No TV for 90 days.

Only G-rated movies or videos for 90 days, and no movie previews.

"Public voyeurism"
Keep your eyes on the road or sidewalk; "bounce" your eyes away immediately if a female comes into your view.

Minimize fantasizing in the car.
Use audio tapes or CD's; and list which ones you will use.

No magazines, catalogs or newspaper inserts in your home that might trigger you.
List those you will get rid of or will ask your wife to get rid of. If any of these are hers and she would prefer not getting rid of them, ask her to put them out of sight somewhere. You are not to look for them.

No reading of personal ads in newspapers or singles' publications.

Establish a defensive protocol when alone at home for 2 hours or more.
Call your sponsor or an accountability partner before or after, in order to eliminate the "dead zones" of time when you're not accountable. Tell them that you have unaccounted for time and what you will be doing to stay out of trouble.

Change the routes you normally drive.
If they bring you close to places that are triggers for you (e.g. convenience stores that sell porn, strip clubs, adult bookstores) then choose another way to go.

No video games with inappropriate images.

Assignment Two – Assessing Character

Men of integrity are men of accountability. They are also men of character.

My favorite description of the life from which we came versus the life to which we aspire is written by Paul in Galatians, chapter five:

The acts of the sinful nature are obvious: sexual immorality, impurity and debauchery; idolatry and witchcraft; hatred, discord, jealousy, fits of rage, selfish ambition, dissensions, factions and envy; drunkenness, orgies, and the like. I warn you, as I did before, that those who live like this will not inherit the kingdom of God. But the fruit of the Spirit is love, joy, peace, patience, kindness, goodness, faithfulness, gentleness and self-control. Against such things there is no law. Those who belong to Christ Jesus have crucified the sinful nature with its passions and desires. Since we live by the Spirit, let us keep in step with the Spirit. Let us not become conceited, provoking and envying each other. (Gal 5:19-26) (NIV)

This is the theme verse of Principle Four. Working on the fruits of the Spirit will be a lifetime journey. In many churches this process is referred to as "sanctification." So, the first thing to think about is that this process won't be completed in this lifetime. There is no way in this assignment that you will be "complete." But you can get started.

Since anger, along with loneliness, is the main emotion that drives sexual addiction, it is not a bad place to start. You will notice how quickly Paul talks about it in the passage above after he has described sexual immorality. He breaks it down into a number of words: hatred, discord, jealousy, fits of rage, selfish ambition, dissensions, factions and envy.

These words are all obviously different, but the root of them all is the same: a wounded heart that is angry about not being loved and nurtured. We all would be so much better off if we just realized that we need to be affirmed, praised, heard, touched in healthy ways, adored and included in a healthy community. When we don't feel that we're getting these things, we can become angry just like a little child who is having a temper tantrum. In fact, there is a lot about your acting out that was very juvenile, exactly like a temper tantrum. Anger and a desperate need to get our needs met will lead to our being ambitious, envious, jealous and competitive. We will have fits of rage, dissensions and lots of discord.

An angry heart is a wounded heart

Anger can come out in a lot of ways. It can be direct. It can also come out sarcastically and indirectly. Sometimes we can get angry at someone who really doesn't deserve it because whatever he or she said or did reminded us of an older wound and an older anger. That older wound and anger may be something of which we are not even consciously aware.

If you find that your anger is really out of control, you may need to work for a time with a Christian therapist who can help you get out the root of it. You may find that simply talking about it with trusted people will help dissipate it. Remember that anger can't be suppressed; it will always come out sooner or later. Writing about it is another good way of expressing it.

Often therapy and support revolves around understanding how we were wounded and feeling the freedom to express anger at those who wounded us. This can be an important part of the journey. It allows us to know that we didn't deserve the things that happened to us.

It is often important to identify who caused us the most original pain. For now, make a list of those whom you know you are angry about. Identify them and write what you are angry with them about. Take a moment and pray and ask God to teach you if your anger is older, that is if your anger at this person is just a reminder of an older wound. One question that I often use with myself is, "How old am I?" This means with any feeling that I might have, how old am I at that moment. You may be surprised that you find that you are very young. One symptom of this would be that painful memories come up for you. If you ask the right questions, memories of the original wound might start entering your mind. Don't be afraid of these. This is a cleansing. Share these memories with your group and ask them for feedback about any anger that you might be having.

When you're sharing your anger at others don't forget about being angry with God. In the pain of my addiction I was often angry with God. I had prayed many times for Him to remove all lustful thoughts and temptations from my life. I wanted to be magically healed or delivered. Even at a young age I was angry that God didn't just zap me and prevent me from all harm. Later, as I grew up and since I became a Christian, I could get angry with God about anything that didn't go right in my life.

> *Write a second list of things that you have been angry with God about. If you're feeling fearful of being angry with God, get out your Bible and open it in the middle. Then read some of the Psalms and see how angry Kind David was with God when he wrote some of those.*

So now you have two lists of your anger to share with your group. What do you do next?

My suggestion is that you think about deciding to forgive every person on your list. You might be saying, "What? You just told me to be angry with them; now you're telling me to forgive them. I don't feel like doing that. Besides, none of them have asked for my forgiveness." Forgiving someone else is for *your* emotional healing, not theirs. You can decide at some point to do it even if you don't feel like it. So often we get this backwards. Our feelings may FOLLOW our decisions, and not the other way around. Another mistake we make is in thinking that forgiveness is a one-time event. You may have to forgive someone over and over again.

Some of us have been counseled not to give up our anger too quickly because if we do, the people who have hurt us might do so again. Don't confuse forgiveness with your ongoing need to set healthy boundaries. You can be safe and not get hurt again.

Forgiving someone is a spiritual act of obedience. It is what Jesus tells us to do. Remember these words: "Forgive us our debts (trespasses) as we forgive our debtors." Do you want to be forgiven for your sexual sins? Practice forgiving others for whatever hurt they have caused you. When you have made a decision to do so, then you must *act* like you have. Remember that you can still have your boundaries, but you can be kind. Now refer back to the fruits of the Spirit that Paul talks about.

> *Write in your journal a decision you've made to forgive someone. Forgiveness is an act of the will. Healing emotions may follow immediately or only after considerable time has passed.*

With God, you, of course, don't need to forgive Him. But you do need to work on accepting that everything God has allowed to happen to you has been for a reason. Just because you don't understand the reason yet doesn't mean that that isn't true. I think back on all the things I was angry with God about. With some of them, I learned some great lessons. Would I take that away? Not on your life.

Reflect on what you have learned from the pain that God has allowed in your life. Write in your journal about some of those lessons if you can. There are a number of great books about this. One that has profoundly effected me is Larry Crabb's *Shattered Dreams.*

Often we are angry because we are afraid. We don't feel safe and we worry about the future. Ours wounds from the past may have impaired our ability to feel safe. We have been offended and abandoned and we have memories of fear and anxiety. We can get triggered back to those. Fear and anxiety feed upon themselves and can really get us involved in a vicious cycle of obsessive thinking about danger.

One of the dynamics that is important is to understand the difference between anxiety and fear. Anxiety is usually about something really large or general in nature – like being totally alone, having no meaning in your life, thoughts about death, and any shame and guilt about being condemned. Fear is usually of something specific. I am generally afraid of not getting my grass cut in the summer and my driveway shoveled in the winter (I live in Minnesota you understand). I can become really obsessed and worried about these things when they don't get done. I can get angry at myself for not doing them or at others (like my two sons) for not helping me. The fact is that taking care of my house symbolizes taking care of my life. A well cut lawn or a well shoveled driveway can help me feel that I am doing a good job of protecting my "space." It sounds silly, doesn't it? But how many of the things that you worry about have been labeled "silly" by others? They are perhaps symbols of deep anxieties that we all have. If you would like to work more on this distinction between anxiety and fear, the *Faithful and True* workbook leads you through it, pages 51-55.

When you begin to understand that even little things can trigger you into deeper anxieties, you can begin to understand why there are times when even little things seem to bother you so much.

> *In the space below, write down the last time you felt really afraid. If you are aware of any words or events that triggered you into this feeling, write those down also.*

If we are really impaired, the antidote may need to be medication for a time. Don't be afraid of this; many people may need this help. Some of us have genetic predispositions in our neurochemistry to have more difficulty with fear and anxiety. That is not something to be shameful of. It is a part of who we are.

Another really important antidote is the safety of the support group that you are beginning to experience. We learn to be afraid in unhealthy relationships and we can learn to feel safe in healthy ones.

During check-in time at every group be sure to report on any fears or anxieties that you are having. Begin to think about what might help you to feel safe. At the appropriate times get some feedback from your accountability group about safety.

The main antidote to fear and anxiety is developing a greater dependence on God. This is a spiritual journey. Refer back as many times as necessary to the work that you need to do in Principle Two and remind yourself of the ongoing discipline that you will need to grow in your relationship with Christ.

Assignment Three – Cultivating Our Character

Now, let us turn to the fruits of the Spirit that Paul describes as love, joy, peace, patience, kindness, goodness, faithfulness, gentleness and self-control. Wouldn't we all like to be more like that? Again, modeling ourselves after these qualities of character will be a lifetime journey. Hopefully, as you continue your journey of healing, self-control will be developing more and more.

One of the keys to the other qualities of character is the ability to be empathetic. **Empathy** is that ability to put yourself in the place of someone else and completely understand what he is going through. Do you begin to see that your addiction has given you an opportunity to be more empathetic? You are beginning to understand your wounds, your pain, your loneliness, your anger and your fear. As you do this you will be better able to understand those feelings in others. You will be able to listen to their stories and understand. You will be more patient, kind, good, gentle and peaceful. This comes from your own humility.

We are in this together. In this assignment I would like to help you in the ongoing journey to develop empathy. Selfishness is, of course, the enemy of empathy. A great question is why is anyone selfish? One formula that I believe to be true is:

Selfishness is equal to unhealed wounds.

Selfish people are those who feel that their needs have not been met. Selfish people are also those who think that only *they* can meet their own needs. This is, of course, an aspect of the original sin, "I control my life; I don't trust God to do it." As you continue to work this program, you will discover more and more that only God can meet your needs. You will also find some of your desires being met by others that you are in an intimate relationship with. You should become less selfish as you learn that there are healthy ways to get what you need.

Empathy begins when you discover that others are just as wounded as you are.

One of the great tasks of recovery is to understand that you are not alone in your wounds. As you sit in your group and listen to others around you, this will become clear. This assignment will ask you to do some rather strange things.

First, pick out one of your accountability partners. Interview him about the wounds that he has discovered for himself. Write a short list of those in your journal. You will, of course, ask him for his permission to do so and you never have to identify him in your journal by name. Be willing to report on this to your group

---

> *Now, pick a member of your family. It may be your wife, a brother, sister, cousin, uncle or aunt, or anyone else that you feel safe with. If that safe person is not your spouse yet, then use someone else. This person should have done some of their own reflection about their own life journey. Do not seek to educate them or convince them of any wounds that they have that they haven't accepted or understood. Interview this person about the wounds they have discovered about themselves. Write in your journal about what you discovered in this interview.*

Let's continue with a rather dangerous assignment by imagining the last person you acted out with. It may be a person in a pornographic picture. It may be a person at a strip club. It may be a person you somehow lusted after. Even if you have the opportunity to interview this person, don't. I want you to imagine now what it might have been like for this person growing up. Let me help you, for example. You do know that the vast majority of women who work at strip clubs were sexually abused as little girls. The same would be true for your average prostitute. Women who pose for pornography have a story of some kind of damage as a child. Remember all of these women are someone's daughter, someone's sister and perhaps someone's wife. Do you see what I mean?

> *In your journal, write a short story telling the life story of that person. What was it like for her, do you think, as a little girl? Remember that you are hearing stories. You are learning how common it is that people have wounds. What is the pain or life challenges of the person whom you chose?*

One of the basic truths about sexual acting out is that you have to objectify that person — that is, imagine them as an object, to diminish any feelings of guilt or discomfort that you might otherwise have.

Now, take another direction. How are you in being affirming and encouraging? Many of us, since we were abandoned of those ourselves, have a really hard time being that way with others, particularly those whom we really love.

You might have to really practice this one. In your groups please try to be affirming and encouraging with each other. When you give any feedback to someone who is sharing, start with an affirmation. Be encouraging before, during and after meetings.

Now, consider those around you whom you love. Who would you say is really starved for affirmation and encouragement? Maybe it is your spouse. Remember that she might not be acting like she needs it because she is so angry or withdrawn. It probably is one of your children, if you have them. All kids need these.

I want you to make a commitment to affirm someone who is close to you everyday and I want you to make note of it in your journal.

Reflect back on a person who was the most affirming and encouraging person in your life. It may not be the person that you hoped it would be, like your mom or dad. Write down their name in your journal. Do you remember how kind and generous and patient and loving you thought that person was? Wouldn't you like to be more like that?

I have seen some miraculous changes in other people when I have simply taken the time to affirm them. Imagine the smile on the face of someone who might just delight in your encouraging words.

You will find that if you carry out this assignment, you will become more patient. All of this is built on what? It is, of course, your ability to be empathetic. Do you see how important that is?

If you find that you have a hard time doing this, go back to the anger section and continue to work on where that is coming from. You will obviously find that your anger comes from your wounds. Do you need to do some more work on those? Remember that there is no shame in therapy or talking to a pastor or close trusted friend.

Study two separate but related scriptures and hear and learn the words of Christ:

Luke 6:27-49
Matthew 7:1-12

Write in your journal any thoughts that you might have about these two teachings.

Finally, remember again that character formation is a lifetime journey. Give yourself an affirmation that after all these years you are finally thinking about these things and taking them seriously.

Principle Five

We explore the damage we have done, accept responsibility and make amends for our wrongs.

Building a Life: I Can Demonstrate Real Change

Principle Five marks a turning point in your journey of transformation. Here's a review of your work to this point as guided by the first four Principles: You admit the unmanageability of your life because of sexual sin and your inability to solve the problem on your own. Next, you choose to surrender totally to Christ and to seek God's will for your life on a daily basis. Inventory your history with complete honesty and reveal the truth through specific confession to another person. Then address your flaws and inadequacies of character by entering into relationships of accountability.

These first four Principles are vital in forming the foundation for genuine, lasting change. You examine the depth of your sinful nature and your need for God. You take the huge steps of telling the truth and asking for help.

The journey this far, though, is also largely self-focused. These examinations and confessions and submission to accountability require great introspection. You're looking inward and exploring your own life, behavior, mind and heart.

Principle Five expands your investigation. It challenges you to look outside of yourself and consider the ways your sexual sin has impacted others. You admit that you're not isolated in your sin and that it has repercussions for others. People in your life are affected by your addiction. Your actions have caused pain for many, probably more than you'd like to think. In a variety of ways, your behavior and character flaws have harmed others. The process of Principle Five begins with a thorough assessment of the damage caused by your sexual sin, its consequences and your character flaws. Like Nehemiah, you venture outside yourself to survey the damage that exists in your environment. You observe the fallout of your life. You catalog the pain you've caused for others. You look unflinchingly at the harm you've brought about.

Assignment One - Assessing the Damage

It may be helpful to think about categories of harm. Examples include physical harm, emotional harm, spiritual harm and financial harm. You might come up with additional ways your sin has hurt others. Prayerfully ask God to show you the truth about your actions and their results.

Remember the reason for exploring the damage: *It's not to increase your despair or add to your shame.* Be assured of this declaration of God's love for you, no matter what you've done:

> *"[The LORD] does not treat us as our sins deserve or repay us according*
> *to our iniquities. For as high as the heavens are above the earth, so great*
> *is His love for those who fear Him; as far as the east is from the west, so*
> *far has He removed our transgressions from us." (Psalm 103: 10-12)*

The purpose of Principle Five is to grow in maturity as you move away from any denial, blame or self-pity and learn to accept responsibility for your actions. As you consider the many ways you've harmed others, you gain a deeper understanding of how your sins have hurt the heart of God. The Prodigal Son (Luke 15: 11-20) provides a perfect example of a sinner who was willing to take full responsibility for his behavior. He understood, too, how his sin had hurt his heavenly Father, as well as his earthly one. **Before you begin the writing assignments, read his story.**

Identify categories of people you have harmed. Examples would include your current family (spouse and/or children), those in your family of origin, friends, coworkers, etc. Be sure to include those who've been indirectly harmed because of your addiction, such as spouses or children of acting out partners, or others who have looked up to you and been discouraged by your sexual sin.

List specifically all those you have damaged. Write each name. Review the categories of people in your life as a guide to help you remember each person. Start with those closest to you, like your spouse and your children

---

> *Describe the nature of the damage next to each person's name. Again, be specific. Following are some concrete examples:*
>
> - *Broke the marriage vows you made to your wife*
> - *Missed important events with your children because of your acting out*
> - *Spent money on sexual sin*
> - *Performed poorly at work*
> - *Gave sexually transmitted diseases to others*
> - *Withheld intimacy from others (or was incapable of intimacy because of woundedness and sexual sin)*
> - *Acted hypocritically by violating your professed Christian standards*
>
> *After the description of the injury you've caused each one, list your character problem that fueled the behavior, like your pride, selfishness, impatience, stubbornness, etc. (If you're not sure about the character defect, postpone this part of the assignment until you've completed Assignment Two of Principle Four, which deals with problems of character.)*

Note: Consider this assignment a first step in identifying those you've harmed. It's not something you can compile one time and be done with. As you grow in your transformation process, you'll identify others you should add to the list. Don't be discouraged if this assignment seems overwhelming or never-ending. It's actually a sign of progress when you become aware of the broader or deeper layers of pain you have caused.

Be sure to be gentle with yourself as you complete these lists. Talk about the process in your L.I.F.E. group. Ask your brothers in recovery to remind you of your worth as a person created in the image of God. Your heavenly Father sent His Son to pay the penalty for the damage of your sin.

Assignment Two - Planning Amends

Assessing the damage as a result of your sexual sin and listing those whom you've harmed is only the starting point. In fact, those acknowledgments are hollow if you stop there. The list you've created serves as the springboard into action – specific, identifiable action. Assignment Two of Principle Five prepares you for taking the actions of *restitution*.

First, I need to define what I mean by making restitution. The Twelve Step programs refer to these actions as making amends for our wrongs. *In simple terms, making amends means offering an apology for the harm you've caused.* It's saying, "I'm sorry," with humility and without any expectation of receiving forgiveness. But making amends is also backing up the apology with specific attempts to make things right. Willingness to provide restitution is a good indicator of the genuineness of your apology.

Addicts can offer two kinds of amends. The first is **direct amends**, where you provide restitution specifically to the person you've damaged. One by one, you approach the individuals who have suffered because of your sexual sin, and you express your remorse for what you've done and for the pain it caused. If there is some overt way to right the wrong, you suggest it, and then provide it if you are allowed.

Zacchaeus, the tax collector mentioned in Luke 19, provides a great example of making amends through specific restitution. He had apparently used the authority of his position to collect more money than citizens owed. After his encounter with Jesus, Zacchaeus promised to pay people back four times the amount he had cheated from them. (See Luke 19: 1-9 for the Biblical account of Zacchaeus' story).

A second type of amends is **vicarious restitution**. This approach is used when it's impossible or inappropriate to make direct amends. Perhaps you don't know how to contact someone you've harmed, or maybe the person has died. In some cases you may not even know the identity of those you've hurt, especially if your acting out has been extensive. These are situations where you can make vicarious amends. For example, you could donate funds to help the victims of sexual sin receive counseling or treatment. One addict I know routinely pays the way (anonymously) for one person to attend a Healing for Spouses program offered through Bethesda Workshops. This addict sees his donation as an on-going way to help others who have suffered, as his wife did, because of their mate's sexual addiction. The possibilities of vicarious repayment are endless.

A second situation that warrants indirect restitution is if it would be harmful to make direct amends. You take this path when it would be more injurious to interact specifically with someone you've harmed. Certain affair situations provide clear examples of cases where it's inappropriate to make direct amends. One would be if the husband of a woman you've had an affair with doesn't know about your involvement. It would be harmful for him to learn about the betrayal through your confession and apology. He needs to learn of the affair from his own wife, not through you. Likewise, it would be wrong to apologize to the children of an affair partner, unless you were certain they were already aware of the infidelity and were old enough to understand your comments.

In these kinds of circumstances, devise some way of making indirect amends to injured parties. Get creative. After all of the thought and energy you've spent figuring out how to hide your sexual sin, put your creativity to positive use and come up with some constructive ways to counteract some of the damage you've done.

Let me caution you about your work on this Principle. It's important you carefully examine <u>why</u> you want to make amends in each case. As addicts, we're used to manipulating outcomes, and it's possible you hope to benefit in some way by saying you're sorry. Maybe you think you'll be let off the hook or get back in someone's good graces. Those are flawed motives that will taint your actions. Refer again to the story of the Prodigal Son in Luke 15. He wasn't trying to regain his status as a son. In fact, he was willing to be a lowly servant to his father. Be unflinching as you examine your heart for any possible selfish motives in making amends. Be courageous.

On the other hand, be optimistic and thankful for the changes God is prompting in you. As you've worked through these principles of being faithful and true, you've progressed from a place of denial to the point of being willing to accept full responsibility for what you've done and the harm you've caused. This difficult work in Principle Five is one more step in your transformation journey. Remember, God will be faithful to finish the good work He has started in your heart (Philippians 1:6).

Examine your motives for the reason behind your desire to make amends to each person on your list. Here are some possible motivations:
to prevent or stop someone from being angry at you;
to make yourself feel better for what you've done;
to influence someone to trust you again;
to manipulate someone's pity or compassion;
to transfer blame by saying, "I'm sorry, but I wouldn't have done this if you hadn't done that;"
to attempt to avoid consequences by expressing regret;
to accept full responsibility for the harm you've caused;
to demonstrate empathy for those you've hurt;
to rectify your damage to the extent possible

Journal about your true motives for making amends in each case. Pray for discernment and purity of heart.

Plan specifically how you'll go about making amends, both directly and vicariously. For each person, first determine if direct amends or indirect amends is most appropriate. Write the best method beside each name. Then develop a plan. Who will you approach first? How will you contact that person? What will you say? What action will you take?

Identify the first three people to whom you can make direct amends.

Then identify three ways of making indirect amends. Write out that plan, too.

Talk with your sponsor and L.I.F.E. group about your list of those you've harmed, the damage you've done and your plan for making amends. Ask for feedback. Are there any obvious omissions to your list? Are your motives as pure as you can make them? Is your plan appropriate and reasonable for the person and situation? Write down any feedback that you received.

Make an appointment to meet with your sponsor or determine when you'll share with your L.I.F.E. group. *Record that time in your journal.* Do not take any action without first sharing your plan with your accountability system.

Assignment Three - Living Amends

Assignments One and Two of Principle Five led you through a process of identifying those you've harmed and creating specific plans for making amends. Now, in Assignment Three, you have the opportunity to demonstrate real change. By taking action in making amends, you will show in overt ways the revolutions that are happening within your heart. For those around you, it may be the first clear example of your "walking the walk" of transformation.

Making Specific Amends

This assignment will consider two broad ways of making amends. First, we'll examine taking **specific actions**, whether directly or indirectly, of making restitution. Making indirect amends is less complicated. After getting feedback from your group, simply take the action. Do it quietly, without fanfare or attempts to draw attention to yourself.

Making direct amends is more risky. Be aware of these **guidelines** about your conversation with someone you've harmed:

- *State the reason you want to talk to this person.* Remember, you've probably hurt this individual in some deep way, and he or she may be wary about talking with you. If you make a specific appointment to meet, explain then why you want to talk. If you haven't contacted someone on your list, but God provides an unexpected opportunity for an impromptu conversation, state in the beginning your desire to express your sorrow at the harm you've caused.

- *Then state clearly how you've hurt this person.* Be specific. General apologies are lame. Instead of "I'm sorry I hurt you," say "I know it was painful when I forgot your birthday because I was absorbed in my sexual sin. I apologize." Be sure to say the actual words, "I'm sorry and I apologize." The mind-set of remorse is too important to let t be merely understood. I believe it's better, though, to avoid asking for forgiveness. It's too easy to be manipulative with a request for forgiveness. If the person extends forgiveness, that's great. But that choice is his or hers and should be made freely without prompting from you. Simply express your sorrow for the pain you've caused and let go of the outcome. You are powerless over the person's reaction.

- *Explain your intention to behave differently and any plan of restitution you'd like to make for the harm you've caused this person.* Again, be specific about what you'd like to do to right the wrong.

- *Listen to the individual's reaction.* He or she may express anger or hurt at what you've done. Be patient and non-defensive. Agree with the harm you've caused and be empathetic to the person's pain.

- *Thank the person for listening to your apology and for expressing his or her thoughts or feelings.*

Don't expect any certain reaction or outcome when you try to make specific amends. Some people won't understand what you're doing and may brush you off. Others may still be too angry to hear you out. Perhaps more will accept your apology. The individual's reaction isn't the issue. *Your willingness to humbly accept responsibility is the key point.* Remember the teaching in I Peter 5: 6: "Humble yourselves ... under God's mighty hand, that He may lift you up in due time." Making amends is as much for you as it is for those you've harmed. It further releases your burden of shame and deepens your trust in God to take care of the outcome when you submit your will to Him.

Practicing Living Amends

The life-long challenge and task of recovery is to live differently, not only in your sexual behavior, but in all areas of your life. By thought, word and deed, an addict must daily observe the principles of being faithful and true. In recovery terms, this kind of practice is called "living amends." In every situation you make the decisions, to the best of your ability, that are beneficial instead of harmful.

A first area of living amends is obviously to maintain sexual sobriety. Without sexual integrity, no other progress is possible. (I'll discuss this concept at length in Principle Six.) Remember the caution that was part of the final assignment of Principle One: this period of time during your second six months of sobriety is a dangerous time for relapse. It's easy to get lax about your recovery efforts. I want to remind you of one important tool of working your program. **Boundaries remain critical to your sexual sobriety**. Review your work on boundaries from Principle One. Are you practicing good boundaries in the physical area? Mental? Emotional? Spiritual? Relational? Don't let down your guard.

A second major part of practicing living amends is following the Golden Rule: treating others the way you'd like to be treated. This goal requires maturity and self-sacrifice. It doesn't come naturally, especially to addicts who have a long history of focusing on their own gratification. A key way this objective relates to Principle Five is in learning to forgive others, just as you hoped they would forgive you when you offered your amends.

Your work this far through this text and with your L.I.F.E. group has put you in touch with some profound areas of your own woundedness. You've identified ways you've been deeply hurt by others, perhaps even some in your own family. You've allowed yourself to feel your feelings of loss, grief, hurt, anger, sadness and loneliness. You understand the ways you've been abused or abandoned.

Principle Five challenges you to forgive those who have harmed you, as well as to humbly make amends to those you have harmed. For some of us, this undertaking is more difficult. Maybe you'd like to nurse your resentments a little longer. Perhaps you've become comfortable in your victim role. Holding on to a grudge lets you ignore any part you may have contributed to the relationship problems.

A clear sign of a changed life course is when you're willing to let go of the dues others owe you. Whether or not the offender expresses sorrow at the pain he or she has caused, you choose to forgive and move forward. You allow God to be the judge and the punisher for wrongs. Paul issues this challenge:

> "Do not repay anyone evil for evil.... If it is possible, as far as it depends on you, live at peace with everyone. Do not take revenge, my friends, but leave room for God's wrath, for it is written, 'It is mine to avenge; I will repay,' says the Lord. On the contrary: 'If your enemy is hungry, feed him; if he is thirsty, give him something to drink.... Do not be overcome by evil, but overcome evil with good." (Romans 12: 17-21)

Don't be discouraged by how difficult it is to make amends to others and to extend grace to others. This will be a life-long process as you grow in your relationship with a forgiving God. You won't do either of these recovery tasks perfectly. Sometimes you won't have the maturity or judgment to even try. Because you're human, you will continue to cause harm occasionally.

Remember our Lord's promise: "My grace is sufficient for you, for my power is made perfect in weakness." (2 Corinthians 12: 9)

Take two specific actions: make one direct amend to someone you've harmed and make some kind of indirect amend. Record what you did in your journal, along with how you felt. Be prepared to share your actions and feelings with your L.I.F.E. group.

List five people you need to forgive. Share the names and situations with your sponsor. Pray together for willingness and help in letting go of your right to avenge the wrongs you've suffered.

Ask your group for affirmations about how far you have come.

Principle Six

In fellowship with others we develop honest, intimate relationships, where we celebrate our progress and continue to address our weaknesses.

Living in Fellowship: I Cannot Succeed Alone

Congratulations on getting this far in your journey to maintain sexual integrity. I know it's taken courage, perseverance and commitment. In many ways it may have been harder than you anticipated. You've experienced many feelings that may be new to you. You've had to humble yourself in admitting the full truth about your history, your thoughts and your offenses. But with God's help, you've done it. You've told your story of sexual sin. You've decided you want to get well and have surrendered your life to Christ. You've accepted accountability from a sponsor and perhaps have begun working with a counselor. You're willing to make amends to those you have harmed. I pray you're beginning to have a deeper sense of God's power and presence in your life.

Principle Six guides you into a way of living that involves genuine connection with others, instead of the isolation you've probably known. The foundation for this work comes from one of my core teaching principles:

Fellowship is equal to freedom from lust.

It's probably hard for you to believe this promise. You may have been alone for years hiding your sexual secrets from others. You've never known the joy of a supportive community. Your shame kept you from connecting with others, while it continued to fuel your lust and sexual sin. (You also probably can't imagine a life free from lust, which has felt like your constant companion for as long as you can remember.) Principle Six offers a path out of your isolation, which in turn, is the road to sexual integrity.

Hopefully, you're already enjoying some of the benefits of fellowship through your L.I.F.E. group. You're bonding with other Christian men who've faced similar struggles and seek to become faithful and true. You're beginning to experience both the grace of God and the grace of other Christians who will love you despite your mistakes.

Assignment One - Practicing the Program

Assignment One of Principle Six covers the basics of cementing this new way of life into daily practice. In this first lesson I'll actually be focusing on the last idea of the Principle itself: "We celebrate our progress and continue to address our weaknesses." I'll outline some specific, behavioral ways of walking the talk of transformation. **This assignment deals with the nuts and bolts of what the Twelve Steps community calls "practicing the program."** Developing true fellowship with others must be built on this foundation.

I'm sure you've become convinced that recovery doesn't just happen. Unless you actually do things differently, your behavior and attitudes won't change. Two slogans from Twelve Steps language describe this reality: *"If nothing changes, nothing changes;"* and *"If you keep doing what you've always done, you'll keep getting what you've always gotten."*

Assignment One details a variety of specific ways to do things differently. I've already mentioned them as part of different discussions from other Principles, but it's important to outline them clearly here. Think of this list as a "paint by numbers" plan of recovery. By this point you consistently should be:

- Caring for yourself physically (adequate exercise, rest, healthy diet, etc.)
- Attending L.I.F.E. group meetings
- Calling someone from your group every day
- Reading this workbook or some other helpful literature
- Enforcing healthy boundaries around your rituals and acting out behaviors
- Practicing honesty with yourself and others
- Taking responsibility for your actions
- Addressing your unhealthy attitudes and character defects
- Accepting accountability from your sponsor
- Participating in therapy if necessary
- Asking God's help for your journey each day

Obviously, you won't be doing each of these things perfectly every day, but this list is a blueprint of goals for your daily life. How are you doing?

The next two pages contain worksheets you can use as a daily inventory to measure your progress. I suggest you make copies of these two pages and put them in your notebook or journal. Each day, evaluate yourself in the five areas described and record your "Inventory Score" as indicated on the chart.

DAILY INVENTORY OF HEALTHY LIVING

Evaluate yourself daily in these five core areas using the scale shown below. The items listed are just suggestions; add others that might be appropriate for you. Give yourself an overall score for each area, then record those five scores on the Daily Inventory Chart.

0	1	2	3	4	5
Doing poorly		Doing somewhere in-between			Doing very well

PHYSICAL AREA	BEHAVIORAL AREA
nutritious eating	sobriety
adequate rest	attending meetings
exercise	calling sponsor/recovering friend
attending to medical needs	healthy work habits
recreation	financially responsible
physical self-care (brushing teeth, shaving)	enjoying a hobby
caring for possessions (living space, car)	avoiding substitutes for sex addiction like smoking, drinking to excess
RELATIONAL AREA	PERSONAL AREA
connecting intimately with someone safe	serene, instead of depressed or anxious
considerate with spouse	receiving counseling
available to children	healing from core wounds
participating in supportive community	aware of feelings and needs
helping others who struggle with sexual sin	reading recovery literature
SPIRITUAL AREA	DAILY SCORE
prayer	Physical area
Bible study	Behavioral area
personal devotional time	Relational area
corporate worship	Personal area
deepening spirituality	Spiritual area

[Total score in each area should be between 0-5.]

DAILY INVENTORY CHART: WEEKLY

	SUN	MON	TUES	WED	THUR	FRI	SAT	**TOTAL**
Physical								
Behavioral								
Relational								
Personal								
Spiritual								
TOTAL								

[Total daily score will be between 0-25. Total weekly score will be between 0-175.]

DAILY INVENTORY CHART: SIX WEEKS

	Week 1	Week 2	Week 3	Week 4	Week 5	Week 6
Sunday						
Monday						
Tuesday						
Wednesday						
Thursday						
Friday						
Saturday						
WEEKLY TOTAL						

Complete the Daily Inventory and record your score on the chart. Continue this practice each day for the next six weeks. Observe the pattern of your scores. Remember, the higher the score, the better. (Think about bowling, instead of golf.) Look at each of the five categories as well as your total score. Are your numbers increasing or decreasing over the days and weeks? If your scores don't show progress, you may be in danger of reverting to old behaviors and attitudes. If that's the case, perhaps you need to revisit the earlier Principles. Share your measurements with your sponsor and L.I.F.E. group each week.

Assignment Two - Changing Our Cycle

By now the cycle of addiction as outlined by Patrick Carnes is a familiar diagram. This cycle outlines the woundedness, which is at the core of our disease, the shame, our preoccupation and fantasy, our rituals, then our acting out and of course, our despair. (Though I doubt I need to remind you about this cycle, you can refer to Assignment Two of Principle One for more details.)

I pray you're maintaining uninterrupted sobriety. I hope you're also experiencing some core changes of life and character. The journey you're making is about so much more than sexual integrity. It's about the transformation of someone who is surrendered to Christ.

Review the commission of Romans 12:

"Therefore, I urge you, brothers, in view of God's mercy, to offer your bodies as living sacrifices, holy and pleasing to God – this is your spiritual act of worship. Do not conform any longer to the pattern of this world, but be transformed by the renewing of your mind."
Romans 12: 1-2

God is after so much more than our sexual purity. He desires our heart. He longs to transform our sinful natures into a closer likeness of His Son.

To illustrate this transformation process, I've created a cycle of recovery, which is shown below.

Laaser Cycle of Recovery

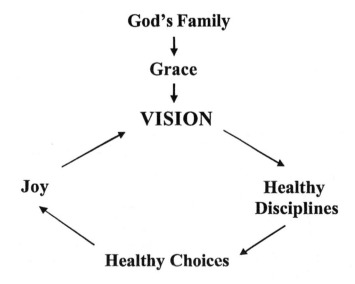

Instead of the addictive cycle of pain and sin, the transformed life of a new creature in Christ is characterized by this cycle of recovery. We will talk about vision in Assignment Three of Principle Seven. Assignment Two, here, focuses on the main body of the cycle itself. It's actually just the visual representation of the behaviors I outlined in Assignment One. The checkpoints that make up the Daily Inventory are the Healthy Disciplines and Healthy Choices depicted in the cycle of recovery.

Review again the five core areas of healthy living that make up the Daily Inventory: physical, behavioral, personal, relational and spiritual. The items listed are examples of healthy disciplines, such as attending a L.I.F.E. group meeting, calling your sponsor or praying. These disciplines lead to healthy choices in behavior, thought and character. Just like there's a predictable progression into sin, there's a known path of transformation. When you allow God to be in control of your life and heart, He can guide you into the pathway of joy as you grow in Him.

Being connected with the family of God provides the fellowship of healthy community. That's why I insist no one can ever recover alone. God made us for relationship, which we obviously can't experience in isolation. We need each other. It's partially through intimacy with others that we come to grow in intimacy with God.

When you live out the Principles of being faithful and true, you invite brothers to be part of your journey of transformation, and you become part of theirs. You dare to admit your sins, ask for help, be accountable, accept responsibility, heal core wounds and share the grace you've found in Christ. In healthy fellowship you find brothers and sisters in the family of God. You tell your secrets, expose your dark heart to the light and live in freedom everyday.

> *Write the names of three to four men who are part of your circle of fellowship. Write a sentence or two of gratitude for each one. Contact each brother this week and share what you've written about your thankfulness for his part in your life.*

List the healthy disciplines you commit to focus on this week. Identify one from each core area you need to improve.

1. Physical	
2. Behavioral	
3. Relational	
4. Personal	
5. Spiritual	

> *Reflect on the positive changes in your life over the last several weeks. Record three or four instances of joy that are evidence of your healthy choices.*

Assignment Three – Growing In Spirituality

The main activity of this assignment is a matter of "conversion." No, not what you're thinking. I do not mean the kind of conversion that changes a person from a non-Christian to a Christian. You've hopefully already done that. I want you, now, to think about converting all the energy with which you used to pursue sex into energy that you use to pursue God.

You know, of course, that the key to this will be **discipline**. This is the ongoing discipline that will be required for you to make ongoing change in your life. Note how the word discipline is from the same root word as "disciple." The word disciple is rarely used in the Old Testament. In the New Testament, however, it is used to refer to a follower of Jesus. Are you that? Then you will need discipline.

You have the energy and the will power. Think again of how much energy you spent being a follower of sex. If you can't remember, go back and review Principle One. If you can't seem to find the energy, you are experiencing some level of shame and depression. Do you remember the category of ritual? Ritual is not a bad word. It is a spiritual one. You will need rituals to follow your spiritual path.

For this assignment we will also need "**enthusiasm**." Enthusiasm is from the Greek. It literally means that God, Theos, is in us. God is in you. Did you know that? Read the entire chapter 15 of the Gospel of John.

Jesus says that He will be in you if you are in Him. He says a lot of other things, doesn't He? How many of you are feeling rather pruned? As you learn to abide in Him you will bear more fruit.

In Assignment One of Principle Six, you started your work on a daily inventory. You were asked to check how you were doing about spirituality in one of the categories. In this assignment, we want you to be much more aggressive in your thinking about this one.

Sometimes when we think about spiritual discipline, we say that we need to have a "quiet time." My experience suggests that many addicts are not very good at that. We are impatient by nature. We don't like doing anything "quietly." For us, increasing our spirituality may be a matter of doing something more active. By that I mean going somewhere to participate in Bible study or corporate prayer or corporate meditation. It may mean going to concerts or seminars where there is Christian teaching on a variety of subjects. It may be putting a cassette into your car stereo and listening while you are driving. We addicts do like to multi-task. There are many different kinds of workbooks that might help some of us be spiritually disciplined. I think of Henry Blackaby's *Experiencing God*, for example. I want you to think creatively, just like you did in your addiction.

For us addicts, another way of describing what we're after is "**quest**." We are on a religious quest to get closer to God. This may involve many active behaviors that we do to find Him. I have known men, for example, who actually travel to places that are of religious significance, like the Holy Lands, as a way of "experiencing God." This kind of quest may not be something that many of you can afford. It is just an example of something active that you can do.

For some of us, discipline or quest may mean doing some act of service. It could be working in the soup kitchen, volunteering for maintenance at the church, visiting in the nursing home or planning a mission trip. We might volunteer for work or participate in a church activity. We might teach a Sunday School class. There is nothing quite like teaching to help you study yourself. There is also nothing quite like trying to explain something to someone else so as to understand it better yourself.

Are you getting the idea? You need to do something. It will probably be something that you have never done before. It could really be out of your comfort zone. You may need encouragement to get it done.

In some church traditions there is a role for "spiritual director." This is a person who directs your prayer life, Bible study and meditations. Has there ever been such a person in your life? In this program, you might originally think of your sponsor as one who can direct you to prayer, study and meditation. In this assignment, you may want to think of another person who can fill this role.

Think "outside the box." The person whom you think about may not be from your own tradition. You might first want to check with a pastor that you know to see how comfortable he would be about this. The key to this role of "spiritual director" is to hold you accountable to those things that you have agreed to do. Your pastor may suggest some men in your church who are willing to take on such a role.

Maybe you don't have a regular church. It could be time to "shop" for one in which you can experiment until you discover the one that you feel really comfortable with.

Finally, here is one last thought. In John 15, Jesus says that there is no greater gift than to lay down your life for another. It is the theme of self-sacrifice that addicts are so terrible at, and healing men are getting better at. Our lust has been selfish. Our healing will be selfless. Think about that as you are wondering what you should do to have more discipline. Whatever it is, it should involve some sacrifice of your time, energy, resources or money.

Write down the name of a person(s) who will hold you accountable to having more spiritual discipline: _____

Write down one act of service to others that you are willing to do: _____

_____

Write down a book or section of Scripture that you are studying:
_____
_____

Write down the name of your favorite spiritual teacher. What books are you reading or what tapes are you listening to? _____
_____

What is your favorite kind of spiritual music? Write down if you go to concerts or listen to tapes: _____

If you participate in a Bible study or group class of some kind, note that: _____
_____

Have you been to any workshops or seminars? _____
_____

What church do you feel the most comfortable in? Write a brief description of why this church feels like home. _____
_____
_____
_____
_____
_____

These are just some suggestions to get you going and keep you going. Remember, there is no such thing as the perfect spiritual program. This is a journey for life. You have already received salvation. This is not about your effort to win favor with God. This is about your time with God and your attempt to get to know Him more.

God's blessings to you in this quest.

Principle Seven

As we live in sexual integrity, we carry the message of Christ's healing to those who still struggle, and we pursue a vision of God's purpose for our lives.

Assignment One - Telling Your Story

The first time you attempt this assignment you should have at least six weeks of sobriety. If you haven't been able to attain this, go back to the Principle One and Principle Four and work on them again. Let's review several things that you need to think about if you are struggling to put solid sobriety together:

1. Are you willing? Do you really want to get well? Is there still a part of you that is resisting the hard work that you need to do?
2. Have you really surrendered your life to Christ? If you haven't, get with a pastor and talk about it some more.
3. Have you confessed your sins totally? Have you really made a complete list of all your sinful sexual behaviors?
4. Have you really put into place a comprehensive accountability group?

Go over your answers with your group or with several men in it. Get some advice as to what AA calls the "next right thing."

This assignment is simple, but it will take you some time. It is a preparation assignment. There are two ways to do it. How you do it depends on your gifts and abilities in life. You have heard a variety of testimonies in your life, like at church or at a meeting. The best ones are relatively short and don't go on forever. It is a greater skill to be succinct. You really have to think about what you are trying to say. You may have done some reading of articles about a variety of things in your life. The typical article in a magazine is somewhere in the neighborhood of 500-1000 words. It is also a greater skill to write briefly, and to summarize your themes clearly and concisely.

For your work here, decide how you feel most comfortable relating your story to others. Do you like talking or speaking, or do you like writing? What do you feel the most comfortable with?

Either prepare a five-minute talk or a 500-1000 word article relating the nature of your story of sexual sin/addiction and what your healing journey has been like.

There are several aspects to include:

Your sexual history. You can include any elements of trauma that you experienced in your family or in your life, but try to keep this brief and generally descriptive, not detailed. You are trying to take responsibility for your own actions and not trying to blame others for what you have done. Be specific of your acting out history, but don't be graphically detailed. You obviously can summarize some behaviors. You don't need to mention the names of any affair partners. Be specific about things like how much time and money you spent on your behaviors.

Describe what you think your efforts to stop were. Make an assessment of why you now think these didn't work.

Describe what your emotions were like during the frustrating times of not being able to find sobriety.

Be honest about any level of spiritual or emotional immaturity you think you experienced.

Detail the day you really made a decision to surrender your life of sin and addiction. Go over any emotions and actions that were a part of this.

What has the journey of healing been like? What have been some of the significant moments in it?

What have you learned about God, yourself and the fellowship of Christ and others?

Now get going. You can use any form of writing – long hand or computer – to write your story. You can use notes or an outline as if you were giving a talk, or you can actually put it on audio or videotape as a way of practicing. You can also ask a friend in healing to listen as you go over it.

When you have done this, report to your group that you are ready.

Assignment Two - Sharing Your Pain

Before you unleash yourself on others, there is one more step that we would like you to accomplish. We would like you to understand what God has been trying to teach you about Him through your story.

We're not saying that God sat up in heaven one day and decided to make you an addict or even to just allow all these crazy things to happen to you. God has allowed us to have free will and to come to knowledge of Him through our own decisions. Amazingly, God has designed life in such a way that our experiences can be used by Him to teach us powerful lessons about what He is really like.

Our job is to listen.

There are many books that you can read to help you with this assignment. I really like the story of the Prodigal Son. You can find that in Luke 15:11-32, but you probably already know the story. I would encourage you to read Henry Nouwen's book, *The Return of the Prodigal Son*. He describes the roles of the Prodigal Son, the father and the older brother.

How is it, do you think, that the father in this story was so understanding of the son? Jesus is telling us, in this parable, that this is what God is like. How is this earthly father able to be so forgiving? Is he not like a lot of other earthly fathers? One interpretation is that perhaps this father had his own sinful past. Perhaps he knew what it was like to make mistakes, and to feel like he was in the "pigpen." Was it out of his understanding of how all of us fall short that he was able to take his son back in such a loving and gracious way? Who would you like to be most like in this story? You already know that you are the Prodigal Son. Wouldn't you also like to be like the father and not the older brother? Is it not your own life experience that might make you this gracious?

There is another of Nouwen's books that we recommend to you. It is called *The Inner Voice of Love*. This gracious and loving man experienced a time of great despair in his latter life. The word is that he, himself, struggled with some sexually sinful behavior. He went off to do a retreat and kept a journal, just as you have been doing. His journal was later published as the book just mentioned.

One of his reflections in that book is very powerful. Nouwen says that we should allow our pain to become "the pain." He believes that all of us have experienced some kind of circumstances in our life that create painful memories and feelings. It is our pain. Nouwen goes on to say, however, that if we only spend time dwelling on the unique circumstances that caused our pain, we will fall short of really understanding it. We might believe, he says, that if our circumstances had been different, we might not have any pain. Better, he thinks to come to an understanding that our pain is our "opportunity" to experience the pain of all humanity.

Think about it. What has connected you with others in your life? Was it success? Has the fact that you have made various achievements really brought you the feeling of peace and serenity that you have longed for? Have you felt connected by being on the winning team? Or, have you felt more connected by getting honest in the last weeks with others who know what you have gone through? It seems to me that when we allow ourselves to know that we are all equal and that we all suffer, we come to true connection. Another book that has affected me a great deal is Larry Crabb's book, *Shattered Dreams*. In it he describes how we come to true connection through our brokenness.

> **Reflect and write in your journal about what your losses and pain have taught you about depending on God.**

Consider these words of Jesus, *"Come to me, all you who are weary and burdened, and I will give you rest. Take my yoke upon you and learn from me, for I am gentle and humble in heart, and you will find rest for your souls. For my yoke is easy and my burden is light."* Matt 11:28-30 (NIV) You have lived that first part about being tired and stressed out. You have sought the rest that Jesus talks about. Has it not been difficult to understand the last part about taking on Christ's yoke? Was His burden really light?

What did Jesus do? Being God's son, He gave up His status and became a man. As a man He experienced many things that we do. He was afraid of death asking God, "If it be Your will, take this cup from me." He felt abandoned in the Garden by His disciples. He was rejected and despised by His own people. He was tortured and put to a painful death. He doubted and wondered on the cross even where God had gone, feeling, "Why have You forsaken me?" He knew the meaninglessness of hell, having descended into it for three days.

When we are in relationship with Christ, we have a brother who knows how we feel. Do you remember what it was like to go to your first meeting, tell your story and feel the huge relief that others understood? When that happened, did your burden feel lighter? That is what Jesus is asking us to do — take His burden, and allow your pain to be the pain of all humanity. It is also His pain and He knows how it feels. Knowing this, would you take your past away if you could? Do you see that perhaps it has allowed you to experience the pain of others? It has given you compassion and empathy for your spouse, your children, your brothers and sisters. Do you begin to believe that it has been a gift? How else would you begin to understand the gift of God's grace through His Son Jesus Christ?

Perhaps, it is time to stop feeling sorry for yourself.

Now, I would also ask you to reflect on any testimonies that you have heard. Which ones have you really been helped and inspired by? Has it been those in which people have bragged about how well they are doing, or has it been those in which people have honestly and transparently told about their struggles and their pain? Perhaps it was a brother who was willing to tell you his story that got you to come to a meeting in the first place.

Would you like to give the gift of your story to someone else? Remember back to all those times when you longed to know that someone else understood what you were going through. Someone came along and now you are on the road to healing. Right now, I would bet that you know someone who needs to hear your story.

Make a list of the names of those to whom you would like to tell your story They don't have to be possible or probable sex addicts. They just need to be people whom you know struggle. As you read this, you may be having a "shame attack." That is, you are saying to yourself, "It will be hard enough to tell my story to other sex addicts. How could I tell it to anyone?" Relax for now. In the early days you will probably practice with those who you know are relatively safe. In the years to come you will find others.

1.

2.

3.

In my early recovery, there were no L.I.F.E. groups or sex addiction groups to go to where I lived. I was advised to go to any kind of 12-step group. So, I chose AA. I started going to a relatively large group and tried to "pass." I'm not an alcoholic so I would just say that I was an "addict." No one seemed to mind at first. Then one of the men asked me, "Mark, just what kind of addict are you?" So, I told him my story. It turned out that he struggled with the same kind of sexual behaviors. Over the next weeks we told our stories to a variety of the men who came to AA. Before we knew it, there were 20 men coming to a sex addict meeting that we started. My belief is that the Holy Spirit will direct your story telling. God will always bring people to you, and you will feel that tug at your heart, that they need to hear your story. Trust your feelings and be of good courage.

Now this doesn't mean that you will rush out and tell your story to everyone. You may have that temptation. Part of you just wants to tell the whole world and get it out there. You might think that this will be a great catharsis, a cleansing of your soul. You will also need to be careful. There are those who might not be safe. When in doubt, always check out your desire to share your story with your group or your accountability network. Get their feedback about safety. They might also be able to encourage you when you need to be encouraged.

Keep track in your journal of those times when you do share your story.

Record your feelings about what it was like. Describe the other person's reaction and what the results were.

Do you see, again, that working this assignment of Principle Seven is a lifetime journey?

Assignment Three - Discovering Your Vision

Having a vision is a familiar Biblical concept. There are countless examples in both the Old and New Testaments of people who had them. Today a vision has become a popular way in which we have talked about having a positive mental image of where we want to go, and of what we want to do.

In this assignment I want you to work on having that kind of positive mental image of where God wants you to go. You may remember that earlier I said that I hope you will be able to replace the fantasies in your life with a vision.

Here is the comparison:

A fantasy is an image of a preferred future in which all of your wounds will be healed.

A vision is an image of a preferred future in which you pursue God's plan for your life.

If you understood assignment two, you may begin to understand how your wounds can be your guides, your teachers, about connecting with God and with others. Your wounds may also become your strengths. You are a stronger person for having gone through what you have.

Now, how do you become a person of vision?

First of all, you must discover and accept what your true gifts are. You might be surprised to find that for years you have been pursuing what others have told you that your gifts are, others like your parents. They may or may not have had your best interests at heart. Reflect on the messages that you think your family gave you about what you were supposed to do in life. My father, for example, never actually told me to be a minister, but he so valued that role that all of his modeling and encouragement was in that direction. Since part of my job was to take care of him, it was also apparent that I was to have care-giving skills. In order to please him, I think, I went into ministry. Don't get me wrong, I now believe that I am truly called to ministry, but it is something I had to claim for myself, not something to do to please Dad. One of my pastor friends says, "I was ordained by my mother and not by God."

> *Think of your family's messages, its modeling and its values. Think of how you were encouraged or discouraged. What is your name? Often those carry significance. What was your role(s) in your family? When you have reflected on all of this, write in your journal what you think your family's mission for you was.*

For example, mine would be simple, "Become a minister and take care of everyone else and not yourself."

It is possible for others to encourage you about your true gifts. First, think of those people in your life who were truly encouraging, affirming and positive. What skills, talents and abilities did they affirm in you? Maybe it was a teacher, a coach, a pastor or a friend.

> *Write down the names of those people and the messages of affirmation that they gave you.*

Now, reflect on those times in your life when you have felt truly passionate about what you were doing. These will be times when you are "in the zone" and feeling that you are doing exactly the right thing. What do you enjoy doing? What has brought you a sense of fulfillment? What has brought joy to the face of others when you were doing it? For what things have others thanked you?

> *Make a list of those times and briefly describe what took place.*

Next, reflect on your education and your life experiences. What has your training been?

> *Make a list of all that.*

Finally, and this is a hard one, reflect again on what you have learned through painful experiences in your life. This will include the most recent ones related to your sex addiction. Pain can be a great teacher and guide. God can speak through hardship. James 1:2 says, "Count it all joy when you experience various trials, for you know that the testing of your faith produces steadfastness."

> *Make a list of all the lessons in life you have learned through your own pain. Remember this could be about loss, failure, hardship or crisis.*

You now have several lists and sets of reflections. Read back over them until a picture emerges of what your true gifts are.

If you've never seen the movie, "The Chariots of Fire," you might want to rent it. It is a wonderful comparison of two men who pursue their gifts and talents for two different reasons. It is the story Eric Liddel and Harold Abrahams, both of whom prepare for the 1924 Olympic games. Both are fast and gifted runners. They both are the best in the United Kingdom in the hundred-meter dash. They both have a dream of winning the gold medal.

Harold Abrahams is the son of a Jewish businessman. He knows that his family has never been fully accepted in English society. Harold Abrahams longs to be accepted. The pain of ethnic prejudice burns inside him. He is an angry man. He concludes that the way to be accepted is to be the world's fastest man, and to "run all of his opponents into the ground." He even hires a coach and trains incessantly. Harold Abrahams does win the gold medal in the hundred-meter dash, but the end of the movie shows that it doesn't bring him joy. It is almost a disappointment.

Eric Liddel is the son of missionaries to China. He is back in Scotland studying to be in ministry and to go back to China himself as a missionary. Eric Liddel knows that his gift is from God. His sister grows concerned that all of his athletic training is distracting him from his "true" work of studying and preparing to go back to China. He takes his sister out on the hills overlooking Edinburgh, Scotland and says to her, "Jenny, I know that the Lord made me for China, but He also made me fast. When I run, I feel God's pleasure." Eric Liddel refuses to run the hundred-meter dash because one of the qualifying races is run on a Sunday. He is switched to the four hundred-meter dash and does win that. He is elated, and has a true sense of joy.

The movie depicted accurately that when Eric Liddel ran, in the middle of the race, he would throw back his head and close his eyes. He literally could not see where he was going. He was a man running with God's help. He didn't need to see where he was going.

What are you doing when you feel God's pleasure, when you don't need to see where you are going?

Make a list of any times when you have felt that you were doing something that brought you pure joy. I once heard Bill Hybels of Willow Creek Church say that hearing the voice of the Holy Spirit will be known by the joy and excitement that you will feel about what you are thinking or doing.

You now have some lists to think about and pray about. This is your own perception and the perception of others about what your talents and gifts are. How does this match up with the expectations you brought with you from your family of origin? How does this match up with what you are currently doing? Don't just think about this vocationally, but in the totality of your life.

Consider this. You worked on the fruit of the Spirit character traits from Galatians 5 in Principle Four. What do you think determines character? Is it a matter of pure will power or is it a matter of vision? Think about it this way. You know that your fantasy life drove your behaviors for years. It led you into traits of character that you have been despairing about for years. Fantasy is a form of a vision. It is a mental image of an outcome that you desire. If that kind of vision is capable of driving behavior and of driving character, would you not also think that a godly vision would drive behavior and character?

My friend and colleague in ministry, Eli Machen, is fond of talking about buzzards. Buzzards have a huge appetite for dead animals. God made them that way. He also gave them a sight or vision capability that is able to see dead animals from hundreds of feet in the air and for miles away. Because of their vision they are capable of flying around and seeing things that we don't see. Buzzards have a buzzard's character and behavior.

Appetite can drive a vision. What is your appetite? Remember the story of the woman at the well of Samaria. She was thirsty for "living water," but she was confusing it with relationships with men. What, again, are you thirsty for? In your old life, you were thirsty for sex. Some of that is instinctual biologically. That appetite will drive you to be attracted to woman and to produce children. God designed men that way too. Spiritually, however, we have an appetite for God. Our problem as sex addicts is that we have confused the appetites. We have merged our appetite for God with our appetite for sex. The great English writer G. K. Chesterton wrote, "A man who knocks at the door of a brothel is looking for God."

We have been thirsty for love, nurture, safety, touch, affirmation and fellowship. We have thought that we could get it through sex. We can only get these things from God. This confused appetite has driven our character and our behavior. We have had a sex addict's behavior and character. It is time to get reoriented.

A vision pursues your appetite for God. If you allow yourself to see that, it will drive your behavior and your character. It will inform your discipline. **Imagine what it would be like to pursue God with the same energy you have pursued sex.**

The next step in understanding your vision is to understand what you would like your legacy to be. A legacy is the influence you leave on others after you die and how you will be remembered. Here are some questions, assuming that you will die before some important people in your life:

1. How would you like your wife to remember you? What will she say about you after you're gone?
2. How also would you like your children to remember you? What will they say about dad at future family gatherings? What stories about you, your character and your behavior will they tell?
3. Who else will remember you when you die? Who will want to attend your funeral and why will they want to be there?

4. What contributions and acts of service will you be remembered for?

Tough questions, are they not? I would suggest that if you can courageously answer them you have a vision of what your true heart desires. Strangely enough, I believe that it will be consistent with what God desires for you.

When you have worked through all of the above you are ready for the last exercise of this assignment.

Write in your journal what your vision or mission statement is. This should not be long — a sentence or two and not more than a paragraph.

As an example, here is mine. "I am to write, teach, speak and counsel for the purpose of educating the Church about sexual health and integrity." This brief statement incorporates what my gifts and talents are, what I have a passion and joy in doing and what I would like to be remembered for.

Men of integrity are men of vision. They know where they are going and what they want to do. If you continue to develop and honor your vision, you will find that all of your behaviors will follow. Remember, again, how your sexual behaviors followed your sexual fantasies.

Before you finish, go back and look at the healthy cycle that I created and that is presented in Principle Six, Assignment Two. My guess is that you have changed a great deal already.

My ongoing prayer for you is that you will continue to grow in strength and faith. Please know that there won't be a day that goes by when all of us with L.I.F.E. Ministries won't be doing that.

The Nehemiah Principles

For this chapter we will need warriors. I have decided to place in a separate chapter 18 principles of accountability from the book of Nehemiah. They were originally placed in Principle Four, but have now been given this place of their own. The feeling is that the book of Nehemiah, and the principles in it, is a great summary of much of the entire workbook. As such, many of the L.I.F.E. groups may want to talk about one of the principles at every meeting.

This work of understanding these principles is not for cowards. It is for those who are willing to take risks.

Before you have a shame attack concerning your lack of courage remember that you have been given all that you need by God. Your job is to find it. It might be as simple as deciding to act courageously.

A reporter once asked a famous British general during the era of the great empire under Queen Victoria, "Why is the British soldier so much braver than others?" His reply was fascinating. He said, "The British soldier is not braver than our enemies; he is simply braver one minute longer."

Are you willing to be braver one minute longer? AA says that we should take it one day at a time. Are you willing to be brave today?

If you are, read the first six chapters of the book of Nehemiah. It has a blueprint in it for accountability. Your job is to seek God's wisdom about how He would have you act responsibly and courageously to defend against the attacks of Satan that would seek to defeat your sobriety.

The story of Nehemiah takes place during a time when the Babylonians had defeated Israel. The city of Jerusalem had been destroyed. Many Jews had been taken back to Babylon to work as slaves. Nehemiah was one of these. He had been given a rather great job, the cupbearer to the King, Artaxerxes. This required that he taste all of the king's drink to make sure that someone wasn't trying to poison him. It was a potentially dangerous job, but he at least got to hang out with the king in the throne room.

In chapter one, one of Nehemiah's brother's, Hanani, comes with other men to tell him about the destruction of Jerusalem. You might expect that if Nehemiah were to be a great leader, he would jump up with a plan to do something about it. As you read the story, however, you see (vs. 4) that when he heard this news, he sat down and wept.

Nehemiah Principle One:

Accountability begins with humility.

You will remember in Principle Two that I stated you must have willingness to find healing and sobriety from sexual addiction and sin. Willingness is about humility. It is knowing that we can't control our own lives. It is about knowing that we need God. Nehemiah is humble. His humility comes from his great sadness.

You may also find humility in your sadness. As you consider the destructive nature of your sexual sins, are you not sad? Sadness is the beginning. Humility reminds you that you can only get well with the help of God. Whatever else the chapter teaches and however basic it may be, if you are not willing to depend on God instead of yourself, you won't find healing.

The rest of chapter one is a prayer that Nehemiah prays to God. In the first part of it he confesses that the Jews have behaved wickedly. You will remember the work that you completed in Principle Three about confession. The second part of the prayer asks God to restore the Jews to their home.

Nehemiah Principle Two:

Accountability depends on honest confession and asking God to restore you to health.

In the opening of chapter two, Nehemiah still does not have a plan. He is still sad. The king notices this and asks him why he looks so sad and gives his own diagnosis, saying, "This can only be sadness of heart." Nehemiah is rather angry and replies, "Why shouldn't I look so sad when the city where my fathers are buried lies in ruins and its gates have been destroyed by fire?" (2:4)

At least Nehemiah is honest. The king responds by asking him, "What is it you want?"

Nehemiah Principle Three

When you get honest about your feelings, someone, even a powerful person, may come to your aid.

So, Nehemiah gets to go home. He has wanted some letters of reference and is ready to go. Know that this is a journey of about one thousand miles through territory occupied by many enemies of the Jews. Nehemiah could make one of the great mistakes that many of us have made in thinking that he could do this alone. However vs. 9 tells us that the king also sent army officers and cavalry with him.

Nehemiah Principle Four

The journey of healing is never traveled alone. You will need the army around you.

In vs. 10 of chapter two you begin to see that the enemies of Israel don't like any thought of rebuilding projects. You know that they are going to come against it. There are vital analogies throughout this book and this is one. So many Christians assume that when they start a healing process and seek to return to the Lord their lives will automatically get better. This passage reminds us that Satan hates any intention that we have to do the right thing, and to rebuild.   In I Peter 5:8 Peter reminds us that Satan is like a lion. He roams around waiting to devour his prey.

Nehemiah Principle Five

Accountability assumes that the enemy wants to defeat us and even more so when we start trying to do the right thing.

When Nehemiah gets home the end of chapter two describes that he goes out at night to survey the damage. It must have been like looking at ground zero after the World Trade Center was destroyed by terrorists. What a terrible sight! The analogy here is that for many of us who seek healing, we might wake up suddenly to all the damage we've created around us. It can be extremely discouraging. The enormity of the task can be daunting. Nehemiah simply starts by gathering everyone and stating in a non-dramatic way, "Let's start rebuilding."

Nehemiah Principle Six

In the face of discouragement and lots of damage rebuilding may simply be a matter of just getting started.

At the end of chapter two the enemies present themselves again. It is a great time for Nehemiah to remind everyone that God is in control and that they belong to Him. He says that the enemies have no historic claim to the people. Remind yourself that Satan has no claim on your life if you are a believer in Christ and that God is in control.

Chapter Three, on the surface, is a hard one. There are so many names to pronounce. It is a chapter mainly about getting organized. The work is divided up into small pieces and various groups get one. That is not a unique principle. It does remind us that if we are to look at the whole project it might overwhelm us. There are many great phrases from AA that might apply here. Obviously, "one day at a time" seems to fit. If we focus on one project or one day at a time, the work may get done.

Hidden in the verses of chapter three are a couple of great principles. In verse 14 we learn that Malkijah gets to repair the Dung gate (that is the NIV translation of the garbage, manure or whatever is involved). Jerusalem had many gates and each one had a function. The Dung gate was the gate out of which garbage and refuse went. It was the Sanitation gate. Without it the city would choke on its own filth. Have you ever been in a city that was having a garbage strike? You will know what I mean. There are many health experts who are saying that the greatest advance of the 20th century was the widespread use of sanitation. It was responsible for ridding the world of more filth and disease than any other medical advance.

The Dung gate is important. One analogy is that you might feel sometimes that your lot in life has been to be involved with Dung. You get the worst assignments, the unimportant tasks, etc. You see that sometimes what seems like the filthy project might be the most important.

There is another great point here. What is the filth in your life? What do you need to get rid of? Maybe it is to get rid of a stash of pornography, take off the Internet from your computer, cancel cable service to your home, or say goodbye to an affair partner. In your journal make a list of those things that you need to get out of your life in order to become sexually sober.

Don't forget that there may be emotions that you need to deal with. They are the garbage of your life. It could be anger, resentments or jealousy. It could be deep hurts from old memories. These may take longer to work on, but for right now make another list of feelings that you need to deal with.

Nehemiah Principle Seven

Accountability means that there will be garbage that you need to get out of your life.

Look at verses 23 and 30. You will read there that these people made repairs to the walls that were across from or next to their own houses. This is an important point. So many of us start getting into what I call "global thinking" when we get into the healing journey. We are finding out so many great and new things that we will want to rush out and tell the world about it. So often many of us have distracted ourselves by helping others and not ourselves. We should be reminded that we need to build close to home. Before we go off too hastily, we should ask ourselves what repairs need to be made to our own homes, to our spouses and to our children. We should be home and be available.

Nehemiah Principle Eight

Accountability means building close to home, taking care of us and our families and not being distracted by all the needs of the world

In your journal reflect on how you have been distracted by the needs of others and not taken care of yourself and your family.

Chapter four is a vital chapter. It begins with a description of how the enemies are marshalling their energies to come against the building project. It would be easy for the people to get discouraged by the threat. Nehemiah deals with it (vs. 9) by praying and by posting a guard day and night.

Nehemiah Principle Nine

Accountability means preparing ahead of time for the attack that you know will come. Preparation starts with prayer and involves preparation that is 24/7.

You simply can't wait for the attack to come. You must prepare for it. This is a great challenge. So many men I have known have fallen because they said to themselves, "When I get tempted, I will call someone or I will do something." That is your pride talking. When you get tempted, a part of the temptation is that you are lonely, angry, bored and lustful. You probably won't feel like calling anyone then, or like dealing with it. You may be into your juvenile entitlement and be saying to yourself that you "deserve" to get some of your needs met.

Let me say it another way: we must prepare in a relative time of strength for the times of attack that we know will come.

You must prepare. This will be at times when your humble self is convicted enough that you want to change and that you want to be sober.

Reflect back on the work that you did in Principle One of this workbook on your ritual. Do you remember the lists you made of behaviors that you will have to stop in order to prevent yourself from getting into your ritual? That is preparation. Let me be clear:

Don't Wait for Temptation

Prepare for It

It Will Come

Do you get the point?

What? Did you think that you have had brain surgery and someone took out all sexual desire from your brain? Did you think that the world has been transformed and that all sexual sin has vanished? Do you think that you are better than other men?

Get humble and get prepared.

You will also notice in chapter four that not only is the guard positioned day and night, it is also placed at the weakest places.

Nehemiah Principle Ten

Accountability means knowing the weakest places of your defense, or your greatest vulnerabilities, and making sure that you have warriors standing with you at those places.

This is not rocket science. When you know your rituals and how you get the most sorely tempted, make sure a number of men in your group know what all of that is about. Ask them to help you prepare for those times. How can defense happen automatically? One basic example is to have men call you everyday. Schedule times during the day when you know you will talk to someone. Don't wait to call them. Have them call you. Most of the time you may talk about the weather. At other times it may get serious and you may discuss whatever is going on. For those of you who travel, in another example, make sure that several men know your schedule and where you are staying. Arrange with them to call you at various times so that you can expect that to happen and not get yourself into trouble. Do you see how this works?

During your group meeting each of you should present what you think are the weakest places of vulnerability in your life. Ask your group to help you construct a plan that is **proactive** in dealing with it.

You will also notice that Nehemiah uses a lot of warriors. It is never just one. Warriors stand together. Did you see the movie "Gladiator?" There is a scene in that movie in which the main character, Maximus, is in the Roman Coliseum. The plan of the Romans is that he and a group of other gladiators are going to be slaughtered in a recreation of the second battle of Carthage. Maximus gathers the men around him and says to them, "Whatever comes through those gates, if we stay together we will survive." As the Roman chariots come in, the gladiators stand together, lock shields and fend off the attack. Maximus continually exhorts them, "Stay as one." Of course they do survive against superior odds.

That is a great picture of accountability. Men standing as one, together. Whatever the world or Satan sends your way, if you stand together, you can survive.

Nehemiah Principle Eleven

Accountability is always in a group of men, not in only one man. If you are only accountable to one person, you will lose the battle.

The most common mistake of accountability by well-meaning Christian men is that they think that they can have accountability "partners." This is foolishness. Have you not been a skillful enough liar to defeat one partner? You need a group of men who really know you and who won't be fooled by you when you are having times of weakness.

There is strength in fellowship. Look at it another way. Loneliness is one of the reasons why you acted out in the first place. Fellowship is the answer. Make no mistake, however, this is fellowship of men who really know you. It is not your average men's Bible study group or church-based fellowship. The guys in your group must really know everything about you. I also feel that, knowing you as they do, they must be encouragers – not disciplinarians. You will respond much better to positive reinforcement. One of my principles is that:

Fellowship with other men who really know you intimately can be equal to freedom from lust.

There is a great battle cry in Nehemiah, chapter four. In vs. 14 Nehemiah says, *"Don't be afraid of them. Remember the Lord, who is great and awesome, and fight for your brothers, your sons and your daughters, your wives and your homes."* (NIV) The great reminder here, again, is that the battle belongs to the Lord. There is much more in this exhortation. Not only does the battle belong to the Lord, but it is to be fought for others.

Nehemiah Principle Twelve

Our motivation to stay sober should be for our brothers and sisters, our spouses and the safety of our homes. This is a selfless motivation. Selfish motivation always fails.

You know that after the great catastrophe of September 11, 2001 we were all greatly inspired by the example of the firefighters and policeman who sacrificed their lives hoping to save others. That is what heroes do. That is what warriors do. You should be no different. Your motivation should be to prevent injuring anybody else around you. It should be to never again see the look of pain on someone's face that is close to you, like your wife. It should be to keep your home safe for your children and others.

If your motivation is to avoid all consequences to yourself and if it is fear based, you will probably fail. Fear only lasts so long. When it subsides you will be tempted to act out again. Motivation that is proactive and based on helping others is usually much more successful. Focus your energy on others. Get out of your selfishness. Be willing to lead a life of sacrifice.

I've had the opportunity to speak to several military groups. What is it that we honor in soldiers? They are willing to die for their country. Would you be willing to die for your children? How about your brothers and sisters? What about your wife? When you can answer yes to those questions, you will be successful in your healing journey.

Here is one last point from chapter four. Notice in vs. 16 and 17 that half of the men built and half stood guard with the spears, bows and shields. Even the men who carried material carried those in one hand and a sword in the other. The picture here is that there was a balance between building and defending, a balance in equal measure. My experience has been that those men who only have a defensive strategy in place get really tired of all the things they're defending against. It takes a lot of energy to defend all the time. Defending is only negative. It is about the things that you don't do. The challenge of this picture is that we must be building something. Our healing must be proactive.

Nehemiah Principle Thirteen

Accountability is about what you don't do, but it is also about what you do.

Positive actions have been discussed in Principle Seven where we talk about the need to ask the Lord to give you a vision. For now, think about some positive action steps that you can do. Some examples might be:

- Eating better
- Getting more rest
- Getting a medical check-up
- Exercising

- Inviting a friend for coffee
- Making a date with your spouse
- Making an appointment with a therapist
- Going to a workshop
- Getting into a Bible study
- Buying yourself some music to play in your car that inspires you. Doing anything just for fun

This is NOT a complete list, just some sample ideas. You will notice that most of it is about self-care, something that you have had difficulty doing. You have been selfish, but you have been providing yourself with false substitutes for excitement, fun and pleasure. You need to start finding the positive ones.

Nehemiah Principle Fourteen

Don't take anything away from yourself if you're not ready and able to put something positive in its place.

I've seen so many programs fail because all the activity of it was negative. Remember that you are probably an abandonment victim. There is a voice inside of you screaming for love, attention and activity. If all you do is to continue to deny these basic needs inside, that same voice will continue to scream. Since you know all of the historically false substitutes, you will probably be more vulnerable to those.

At every L.I.F.E. group meeting share something that you have done that week for yourself that is positive. This should be a part of your check-in.

In chapter five of Nehemiah we see that the work is getting tiring and expensive. The strength of the workers is giving out. There are those around extracting various taxes and expenses. They are making a profit. Some of the people even go so far as to sell their own children into slavery.

In my own first year of recovery I went to therapy and support groups all the time. I was scared enough to go to something almost everyday. It was expensive and it was tiring. I remember thinking during that time, "When does this end, when does it stop, and when do I get to stop being an addict?" Pat Carnes discovered in some of his early research about sex addiction that the period between the sixth and the twelfth months of healing is the most dangerous time for relapse. It is for all the reasons of being tired. It is also because in the first year not all consequences have gone away and life hasn't necessarily become much better. During this time, any of you might be tempted to go back into slavery.

Read chapter 5 verse 13. Nehemiah says, "I also shook out the folds of my robe and said, 'In this way may God shake out of His house and possessions every man who does not keep this promise. So may such a man be shaken out and emptied!' At this the whole assembly said, 'Amen,' and praised the LORD. And the people did as they had promised."

Nehemiah Principle Fifteen

Doing the work of healing will be expensive and exhausting. God is sufficient. Don't sell yourself back into slavery. KEEP YOUR PROMISES!

Say "Amen."

Now, this principle is just a reminder that when you think you can't go on OR you think that you're done or that you're healed, you're not. Keep reaching out for help and support.

In Nehemiah, chapter six, the wall is nearing completion. The enemies are getting frustrated with any frontal assault and so they come up with three different schemes to defeat it that are much more subtle.

The first one is that they invite Nehemiah to a meeting outside of the city. They are plotting to kill him. One way of looking at this plot is that it is the plot of 'distraction." I'm sure that the enemies were acting polite and civil and it seemed like a rational thing to do to have a meeting. The analogy here is that Satan will come after you with very subtle, civil and rational sounding distractions. It may simply be something like, "You've been working so hard, why don't you take a break. Come to a meeting." The form it could take is that of your own self-talk, "I'm tired, why do I have to spend so much energy working all the time? My boundaries are so intense, maybe I can relax a little." Remember that you may be also tempted to stop being such an "addict." Maybe it is OK to go into that video store, you're only there to pick up a Disney video for your kids.

This is subtle spiritual warfare that you're dealing with. I want you to hear the words of Nehemiah when he says, "I am carrying on a great project and cannot come down." Never lose sight of the great work that you are doing and never waiver.

Nehemiah Principle Sixteen

Temptation comes in many disguises and many voices, including your own. Never waiver from the great work you are doing.

On the day I am writing this I had breakfast with a long time friend of mine who has been sober now for 20 years. He told me about a new meeting that he had just started and that he was going back to all the basics of doing all the work all over again. I got the impression that this is a healthy way of life and that he wouldn't change a thing. Neither he nor I have fallen into the dangerous trap of thinking we have "made it," "we are healed," and "now we can let down our guard."

The enemies step up the attack as chapter six continues to unfold. They circulate a rumor that Nehemiah is trying to usurp the power of the king. They are still trying to get him to the meeting so that he can discuss these rumors. The enemies are basically saying that Nehemiah is trying to be too powerful and is too full of himself. They are accusing him of grandiosity.

This can happen to you. There will be voices, people who wonder about what you're doing in your program. Are you trying to be something that you're not? Many of these voices will be secular ones. They will taunt you with being "self-righteous" about your sexual morality. In an article in "Playboy" magazine, I was accused (along with others) of inventing the concept of sexual addiction so that I could make money treating it. The assumption was that sexual addiction doesn't exist. At other times I have been accused of being too "moralistic," and full of myself, or just plain wrong about my definitions of morality. These can get really tiring and sometimes frightening. You will often be misunderstood about your feelings and motivations.

These false accusations against Nehemiah are the same kind of rumors that Jewish leaders circulated about Jesus. They said that He was trying to be King. They dragged Him in front of Pilate and accused Him of being a radical and a revolutionary. Pilate knew it was crazy and thought he had it solved when he stood Jesus next to Barabbas and asked the people who they would chose to have him let go. Barabbas was a revolutionary and Pilate must have thought it was a way to "wash his hands" of the matter and get the people to do his work for him. Of course it backfired to our glory and salvation.

My point is that you will deal with misunderstanding and perhaps false rumors.

Nehemiah Principle Seventeen

Accountability doesn't depend on being fully understood. You may be accused of being proud and arrogant for your morality. It will feel lonely, but remember you are about a great work.

Nehemiah says that the enemies are making all of this up in their head. He knew that they were trying to frighten him and the others. Nehemiah simply prays that God will "strengthen their hands." There will be times when you need to pray for strength and find the support of those around you who are willing to encourage you in the ongoing work.

There is one final plot. An invalid by the name of Shemaiah invites Nehemiah to come with him to the temple where they will be safe. The work is dangerous he says, better to be safe. Nehemiah's response is powerful and he says, "Should a man like me run away or try to save his own life?"

Nehemiah Principle Eighteen

You will need to take risks. That means being willing to sacrifice even your own life.

Read Ephesians 5:2. Paul says that we should be willing to be like Christ, to give ourselves up as a "fragrant offering and sacrifice to God." We won't be perfect at doing that in this life. Only Jesus could really do that for us. In Ephesians 5:1, however, Paul starts by saying that we should be "imitators" of God. We can try. Sacrifice can mean taking risks to do the right thing, even if it makes us feel afraid.

I have gone to such length to teach these 18 Nehemiah principles because accountability will be the core of your program for the rest of your life. This is not just because you are a sex addict. This is because you are a man and seek to follow Christ. My friend Steve Arteburn has written a book, *Everyman's Battle*. It is all of our battle. Surrender your shame to God again. We are all sinners and fall short.

Before we finish with Nehemiah, just notice at the end of chapter six how long the building project takes. It is only 52 days. Remember during those times when you are tired and lonely and frightened that you are doing a great work and that some good things may start coming to you in a shorter time than you might imagine.

Your understanding of this chapter will mean that you should have identified at least four or five men who will be willing to stand with you. These men know all of your acting out behavior, all of your rituals, all of the ways you have fantasized and all of your emotional history. Checking in with them won't take long because they know you so well already. When you do check in with them they will be able to quickly give you feedback about what you should do to protect yourself in the days to come. These are the warriors who will be standing with you in the gap against all attack.

Try doing this, particularly in your first few months of recovery, everyday. In your journal, or in this workbook, attach a phone list of every man in your L.I.F.E. group who really knows you. Make sure you are willing to call one of them everyday.

---

[i] Mark R. Laaser, <u>Faithful and True</u> (Zondervan, Grand Rapids, MI) 1996: <u>Faithful and True</u> (workbook) (Lifeway Press, Nashville, TN) 1996.
[ii] Mark R. Laaser, <u>Faithful and True</u> (workbook) (Lifeway Press, Nashville, TN) 1996

Printed in the United States
698100003B

9 781591 602538